A Soldier's Perspective

1916-1919

BY

Carol Ann Asplund

DORRANCE
PUBLISHING CO
EST. 1920
PITTSBURGH, PENNSYLVANIA 15238

Dorrance Publishing Co
585 Alpha Drive, Suite 103
Pittsburgh, PA 15238
Visit our website at www.dorrancebookstore.com

ISBN: 978-1-6495-7203-5
eISBN 978-1-6495-7711-5

Chapter 1:

Walter C.R. Krieger's Early Life

In 2018 as I unpacked my boxes after moving into a condo, I discovered a Worcester, Massachusetts, newspaper from 1918 with my grandfather Walter's photo on the front page and an article relating how he had been wounded in France during WWI; and his brother Eugene had also been wounded there but more seriously. While unpacking more boxes about a year later, I found my grandfather's WWI diary written in 1918. Later I discovered three more diaries: one from 1916 in New Mexico, and two from 1917 and 1919 on his military service in France.

As I read this, it seemed like he was speaking directly to me. I remembered my life with my grandfather Walter Krieger with whom I lived most of my childhood. I remembered him telling me of his service in the southwest during Poncho Villa's raids and how he was wounded in France in WWI. He showed me his purple heart that he was awarded for bravery in action and for being wounded in that war. An account of his life and, especially, his perspective as an American soldier in 1916-1919 in World War I follows.

• ..

Walter as a Baby

Walter Charles Robert Krieger was born on November 30, 1894, in Jersey City, Hudson, New Jersey, of German heritage. His brother Eugene was born three years later on December 29, 1897. His father, Eugene Rudolph Krieger, was an artist who designed wallpaper. The family moved to Worcester, Massachusetts, in order for Walter's father to work for a wallpaper manufacturer, named Preager Wallpaper, on Neponset Street. Walter's father was born on May 7, 1873, in Manhattan, New York City. His mother, Matilda Ackerman Krieger, was born on September 1, 1876, in Union Hill, Hudson, New Jersey. Walter's mother, Matilda Ackerman, died of quick consumption in Worcester, Massachusetts, on March 27, 1903, when Walter was eight years old and Eugene was five years old.

Walter (eight years old) and Eugene (five years old)

Walter's father needed a woman to raise his two sons, and in 1904 married a Swedish woman named Esther Dahlgren who lived in Worcester. Esther was born on October 11, 1879, in Karlstad, Varmland, Sweden. Together they had another son, Edward, on July 27, 1905. She passed away on September 7, 1912, in Worcester, Massachusetts. Walter had already left home on April 7, 1911.

Photo of Walter and Edward (his half-brother)

Walter met Norma Evelina Kjellberg by association with the Swedish community in Worcester, Massachusetts, and perhaps by working at Norton Company in Worcester, Massachusetts. Norton Company manufactured ceramic crocks when first in business, and later manufactured grinding wheels and abrasives at present. Walter was a machinist and Norma was a secretary.

Norma had been born on March 19, 1894, in Worcester, Massachusetts. Her father, John Johansson Kjellberg, was born on January 8, 1858, in Stenestad, Malmohus, Sweden, and died on December 8, 1943, in Worcester, Massachusetts. (He changed his surname from Johansson to Kjellberg upon immigration to the United States as he started a business as a cabinet maker, patent maker, and house builder.) Her mother, Mathilda Frodigh, was born on August 18, 1855, in Hoganas, Malmohus, Sweden, and died on August 17, 1938, in Worcester, Massachusetts.

Below is a baby photo of Norma

Photo of Norma (age four) and Erhard Kjellberg (age ten)

Norma has a white hat and Walter is in the middle while dating, with her brother Erhard on the right.

Norma's brother, Erhard Kjellberg, was a friend of Walter's. Helen Sawyer, who worked for Norma's family, later married Erhard. Walter and Norma started dating on January 1, 1916, and became engaged on July 19, 1917. The last time Walter saw Norma before going to fight in France was on September 29, 1917, until he returned from France in February 1919. Walter's military service began during the war with Mexico as follows.

Walter on left and Norma in the middle with a white hat while dating, with Erhard to the right of Norma

Chapter 2:

Walter Volunteers
for the Mexican Expedition

During the Mexican Revolution of 1910 to 1920, Francisco "Poncho" Villa decided to attack the United States on March 9, 1916. His forces attacked Columbus, New Mexico, to get supplies. According to Wikipedia, the United States originally termed the war as the Punitive Expedition, U.S. Army, but it is now known at the Mexican Expedition. General John J. Pershing was sent to conduct the expedition. Walter joined the Army in 1914 at the age of twenty and served in Texas, New Mexico, and Mexico in 1917. The war was unsuccessful as Poncho Villa continued to evade U.S. troops. However, the troops stayed until February to prevent Mexican troops from further attacks across the border into the United States. The war ended on February 7, 1917.[1]

The following is from Walter's diary from 1916 when the Massachusetts National Guard was called to serve in the Mexican Expedition:

6-9-1916 First call to colors of the Massachusetts National Guard.

6-19-1916 The National Guard left Worcester to Framingham, MA. We remained at Framingham for orders to move. Meanwhile we had drills and inspections.

6-26-1916 The National Guard left Framingham, MA for New Mexico at 6:45 P.M.

6-27-1916 We arrived at the station at 2:00 A.M. and boarded the train at 3:00 A.M. We passed through Rhode Island and Connecticut.

6-28-1916 We passed through Poughkeepsie, New York at 4:00 P.M. We stopped at Maybrook, New York for morning exercises.

6-29-1916 We passed through Pennsylvania and Ohio into Indiana. We went swimming in the Wabash River. We passed through Indiana into Missouri.

6-30-1916 At 11:15 A.M. we crossed over the Missouri River. We went through Kansas and Oklahoma into Texas.

7-1-1916 We traveled through 600 miles of desert in Texas.

7-2-1916 At 6:45 P.M. we arrived in El Paso, Texas and were ordered right to Columbus, New Mexico which is the town that Poncho Villa attacked on March 8, 1916 burning army barracks and robbing stores.

7-3-1916 We arrived in Columbus at 2:30 in the morning. We slept on our rolls until it was light enough to pitch the tents. We were all tired out.

The above photo is of Broadway in Columbus, New Mexico. This and the following photographs are courtesy of Ellen (Asplund) Racine, curator of the Northborough Historical Society. Photos were taken by Clarence Nelson, who was in the same Company A as Walter.

7-4-1916 We slept and stayed around the camp all day.

7-5-1916 We were supposed to have inspection at 2:00. Inspection was called off by a big sand storm.

7-6-1916 Inspections were called off on account of getting new uniforms.

7-7-1916 We stayed around our quarters all day and were in the Outpost at night.

7-8-1916 We got in from the Outpost at 6:30 A.M.

7-9-1916 Nothing was doing all day until retreat at 6:00 P.M.

7-10-1916 It rained all day, so we have mud all over our shoes. There were no drills.

7-11-1916 After we cleaned up today, we had two hours of drill. It's nice and cool.

7-12-1916 I reported to Western Union as the dispatcher for the Military Service. For dinner we had hamburg steak, spuds and peas. My experience with this detail is very interesting. I delivered Telegrams to General Pershing, Colonel Slocumb and General Herring. We received all messages from Base Headquarters also.

7-25-1916 Company A of the 2nd Massachusetts Infantry was at Retreat.

The photo below was provided by Ellen (Asplund) Racine of the North-borough Historical Society.

Photo of Sergeant Clarence Nelson who took many of the photos and provided some narrative

Walter's photo of Co. A 2nd Mass Infantry July 25, 1916

8-9-1916 I was relieved off of messenger service back to the ranks with my company which is Company A, second Massachusetts Infantry.

8-10-1916 I took a day off to get rested for the hike. We started at 3:00 P.M. for the range with full equipment on. We arrived at the range about 6:30 and pitched our tents. I went for a walk up on the mountains and captured a rattlesnake when it was almost dark. It measured about four and one-half feet long. I arrived back in camp about 10:30 P.M.

Photo of Walter with rattlesnake.

8-11-1916 We had shooting in Platoon formation. I shot forty-three out of a possible fifty in the morning. In the afternoon I went for another hike to the mountains. When I returned, we started out for Outpost duty, arriving at the Outpost at 6:30 P.M. It was a beautiful night with the moon out all night. It was almost as light as daytime. I acted as Corporal of the Guard from 6:40 until 11:00 P.M.

8-12-1916 I arrived back in camp at 6:20 A.M. and fell in for mess. I slept a little. We had inspection of our rifles at retreat which was 6:00 P.M.

8-13-1916 In the morning we had an inspection of our feet, etc. In the afternoon we were ordered to the ball game. We would be put into confinement if we didn't go.

8-14-1916 We had drill from 7:30 A.M. to 11:30 A.M. During the afternoon, we went to town where we did a little shopping until 3:00 P.M. We fell in for a bath. At 5:15 P.M. we had mess and retreat at 6:00 P.M. During the evening, we had a parade. It rained hard all evening with lightning and thunder.

8-15-1916 In the morning the weather was cloudy with rain. Drill was from 7:30 A.M. until 11:45 A.M. Mess was at 12:10. School was at 3:00 P.M. Mess was at 5:00 P.M. Then I hiked to the Outpost.

8-16-1916 At 6:10 A.M. I returned from the Outpost. I rested in the morning until mess which was at 12:00. Drill was from 3:00 P.M. to 4:00 P.M. Then we had retreat. I got a mysterious postal from a party in Worcester named Floradora. I received a battery and a letter from Norma and a letter from Mrs. Erlandson.

8-17-1916 The weather was cloudy. Drill was from 7:30 until 11:30 extended and close order drills. We had skirmish drills and guarding corrals for the horses in case of attack. Mess was at 12:00 A.M.

Walter in New Mexico airing out tent

8-18-1916 The weather was 110 degrees and somewhat cloudy. Drill was from 7:30 to 11:30 A.M. We had skirmishes and close order drills. The Company fell in for showers and a bath. The Regimental Guard was on first relief guarding picket lines near the corrals – two hours on and four hours off. It's a fine day with a little breeze. I wrote a letter to Mrs. Kjellberg for her birthday.

The photo below of Sergeant Miller guarding the horse corral was taken by Clarence Nelson and provided by Ellen (Asplund) Racine of the Northborough Historical Society.

8-19-1916 I was on Regimental Guard all day with two hours on and four hours off. It is a fine day with a little breeze. Mess in the morning was hominy [corn grits] and coffee. We had potato stew and coffee for dinner and beans and tea for supper. I got a letter from Norma.

8-20-1916 Morning mess was pancakes and coffee. We had morning exercises, inspection of our feet etc. and then a shower and bath. I walked about eight miles and saw lots of things, but was caught in the rain while coming back. It rained all afternoon. Dinner mess was roast beef, potatoes, string beans and butter. Evening mess was prunes and apple pudding with tea and a piece of cheese as big as a quarter. I was at the Outpost tonight. [I'm not sure how they set up showers and a bath for the troops. Walter did not say. Maybe they improvised a tank of some sort and filled it with water or hitched up a hose of some type.]

Photos taken by Clarence Nelson courtesy of Ellen (Asplund) Racine, curator at Northborough Historical Society

8-21-1916 I came back from the Outpost and it rained from 12:00 P.M. continually until 4:00 A.M. Mess was cornwilly hash, prunes, bread and coffee. I slept in the morning. Noon mess was hamburg steak and spuds with tea. I had the afternoon off. Mess was tomato stew, bread, butter and coffee. We had an evening parade. There was a heavy wind and rain started about 7:30 P.M. It blew down a lot of tents. I got a postal from Grandpa.

[Cornwilly is corned beef hash fed to the troops.]

8-22-1916 We had morning exercises at 6:00 A.M. For mess we had two slices of toasted bread fried in eggs and coffee. Morning drill was from 7:30 A.M. until 11:30 A.M. We had skirmishes and close order drills. I was detailed to keep the incinerator going. Dinner mess was cornwilly hash, potatoes, one piece of bread and coffee. During the afternoon, I went horseback riding to snake hill which is a distance of eight or nine miles. I got caught in a hard rain on the way back and arrived in camp about 5:00 P.M. For mess we had beef stew, bread and coffee. There was no retreat or parade on account of a heavy rain. Some floods filled up all the ditches around the camp. I received a bundle from the Norton Company, consisting of many things to eat and smoke. I also got a box of writing paper with forty-eight stamps and a pencil.

8-23-1916 The weather was rainy until 7:00 A.M. For mess we had salmon and potato, bread and coffee. Drill was at 7:30 A.M. with skirmishes and close order drills. We had bayonet exercises for half an hour. The drill field was very muddy. This morning I received a magazine from Norma and a letter from Dad with a check for ten dollars. For noon mess we had steak, spuds, onions and coffee. During the afternoon, we went to town shopping and I also had my shower and bath. For supper mess we had pancakes and tea. I am on Guard Mount tonight starting at 6:00 P.M. There's a thunderstorm approaching this way across the desert. I am stationed as Guard in the Sentry Box around the Bull Pen – two hours on and four hours off. It rained hard for one hour steady.

8-24-1916 I am on Guard Mount all day. For morning mess we had beans, bread and coffee. The weather was very cloudy in the morning. I was detailed on the incinerator. Our dinner was hamburg steak and spuds with coffee. I guarded a prisoner to his mess. It started raining about 5:15 P.M. so it was muddy and sloppy walking. I ate my supper by candlelight. I had cornwilly hash, bread, tapioca pudding and coffee.

8-25-1916 It's sloppy and muddy in our Company's street. Morning mess was oatmeal, bread, tapioca pudding and coffee. For the morning we had skirmishes and a bayonet drill with a talk on making trenches. We finished the morning's work with a manual of arms. Noon mess was cornwilly stew, bread and coffee. At 2:15 in the afternoon we started for the range which is eight miles from camp. We arrived at the range at 4:25 P.M. with two rests of ten minutes. For supper we had beans, bread and coffee. After mess, we pitched our tents. It is a beautiful evening – no wind at all. I received a letter from a Pal in San Antonio, Texas and one from Norma.

8-26-1916 We had morning exercises. Mess was oatmeal, bread and coffee. I went on a hike all alone and caught a rattlesnake with seven rattles. I almost got bitten, but by luck, I got him right in the center of his head with my bayonet. I also climbed to the very peak of a mountain for a distance of three miles high for a century plant. I finally got one. I saw one that was in blossom – they blossom every one hundred years (hence the name). It's a beautiful day today. For noon mess we had cornwilly hash, bread and coffee. We spent the afternoon practicing shooting. I scored forty out of fifty. We left the range for the camp at 4:25 P.M. and arrived at 6:09 P.M. It was record time to date. I was pretty tired when I struck camp this evening. I had a nice pint of chocolate ice cream and a bottle of root beer. This ends my day's diary. Tomorrow is coming soon. I will now jump into my little cot and sleep like a top.

[The century plant is a type of agave ten feet wide and six feet high with a tall central shoot of yellow flowers native to Mexico, New Mexico, Arizona, and Texas.]

Soldiers catching rattlesnakes on the mountain (Walter is seated on the far right holding the snake)

8-27-1916 After morning exercises, we had a breakfast of bacon, spuds and coffee. Instead of drinking the coffee, I made myself a nice cup of cocoa. I went to town and got shaved and my shoes shined. We had inspection of our feet, etc. I skinned the rattlesnake I killed yesterday. For noon mess we had beef steak, spinach, potatoes, bread and coffee. During the afternoon, we went into town to see the circus Cole Brothers. It was some circus. I had a banana split and a piece of watermelon. Our Company fell in for a bath. Retreat was at 6:00 P.M. For evening mess I had three biscuits and one hard-boiled egg. Instead of the coffee I made a nice cup of cocoa. I dropped a postal to Gramps, one to D.M.A. and one to Norma, as well as a letter to her. We had a nice line in review. It's raining off and on this evening.

8-28-1916 After morning exercises, we had pancakes and coffee for mess. For morning drill we had skirmishes. Noon mess was roast beef with onions, sweet potato, and coffee. I sent a bundle home for twenty-seven cents. We went to the circus again in the afternoon where I had some ice cream. For evening mess I had a piece of bread and coffee. Mess was some kind of "slop" but I didn't eat it.

8-29-1916 We went on Outpost duty and had the last half on patrolling every hour until 5:00 A.M. For breakfast mess we had shredded wheat, milk, cantaloupe and coffee. I slept all morning. Noon mess was cornwilly stew, bread and coffee. I didn't eat the stew. They served punk for dinner. I went to the canteen and got a quart of ice cream. They bought the canteen out of pretty nearly everything. I looked over all of my property, including letters etc. They have got a new system for mail now, no first class mail. The privates drill in the afternoon. One of our men deserted last night with the circus. His name was Stephen Baker. We had retreat but no parade on account of a coming storm. We hurried to put our tents up in good shape. We no more than got them all fixed when down came the rain in buckets, flooding the Company streets in great style. Our evening mess was cornwilly pie with bread and coffee. I got a letter from Norma and felt somewhat relieved.

8-30-1916 We had morning exercises in the rain. For mess we had oatmeal, cantaloupe and cocoa. It was a fine breakfast. It was raining while we were out at drill: we had skirmishes and close order bayonet exercises. For noon mess we had frankfurts, sweet potatoes, bread and coffee. In the afternoon I wrote to Norma and then went up to town where I got shaved for muster. For evening mess we had cornwilly hash, bread with jam, bread pudding and coffee. In the evening parade we had a fine line in the review. We got new shelter halves. I went to see Gene in the hospital. Afterwards I went to the moving pictures. When I came back, I dropped into the Y.M.C.A. and mailed the letter to Norma. I played pool for a few minutes. After I came back to camp, a postal was waiting for me from Dad and Eddie. I turned into my tent to get some sleep.

8-31-1916 For morning mess I had two eggs, bacon and potatoes. We had muster all morning. Noon mess was meat, beets, potatoes and coffee. The Company fell in for their last bath at the old camp. We are getting ready to move. Evening mess was beef stew, bread and coffee. I had the last half of duty at the Outpost.

9-1-1916 I came back from the Outpost at 6:00 A.M. We fell in for breakfast of shredded wheat, bread with jam and tea. I got a letter from Eric Bergstrom. Today we moved to the new camp site three miles distance inwards. We worked very hard with pick and shovel. We took down the tents and pulled up the tent pins. I helped take down Company C's tents. I left the old camp at 3:00 P.M. and hiked to the new camp. After we got to the new campsite, I was detailed to put up the Company C's tents and Headquarter's tents. Our noon dinner was frankfurts, beans, bread and coffee. For evening supper we had cornwilly hash, biscuits and tea at 6:45 P.M. This ends my day's work and I feel all tired out.

9-2-1916 After morning exercise we had mess of oatmeal, bread and coffee. I was detailed to Lieutenant Knight for loading lumber on trucks and was relieved at 11:00 A.M. I went over to the canteen and got a can of sardines, Fig Bars, and Zu Zu ginger snaps. I also had three ice cream cones. The weather was very cloudy today, but no rain. For noon mess we had a good old fashioned boiled dinner with bread and tea. Jewell and I were detailed all afternoon until 4:45 P.M. to lug dirt and shovel dirt for the new mess hall. For supper mess we had salmon, potatoes, and bread. For retreat and evening parade we were under battalion review. I got a letter from Norma and Mrs. M. Hall. I am now going to retire for the night.

[Zu zu ginger snaps were round drop cookies a combination of ginger and sugar-cane molasses.]

The photo of the 2nd Massachusetts Infantry below was taken by Clarence Nelson and provided by Ellen (Asplund) Racine of the Northborough Historical Society. It shows the water supply of the 2nd Massachusetts infantry.

9-3-1916 After morning exercise we had a breakfast of beef and potatoes. I was detailed as room orderly for today. Then I was detailed to Headquarters to fix the tent for Catholic services. After shaving and cleaning up, I rested for about two hours. Noon dinner was meat, potatoes, onions, bread, doughnuts and tea. I also had two ice cream cones. Afterwards I cleaned my rifle. Our Company is on Regimental Guard. We rolled our packs for inspection. For supper we had macaroni and tomatoes with coffee and a piece of cake. Our Company didn't parade on account of our detail. I filled the water tank. We had feet inspection in the morning. Today's weather was clear and warm with a little breeze. I wrote a letter to Mrs. M. Hall and received a letter from Maurice Fitzgerald. This finishes my day's work. Now for the cot.

The following photo of foot inspection by Clarence Nelson courtesy of Ellen (Asplund) Racine, curator at Northborough Historical Society.

9-4-1916 Labor Day. After morning exercise, we policed the street. Inspection was in the field by the Colonel. I rolled up the Captain's walls on his tent. For morning mess we had oatmeal, bread and coffee. Noon mess consisted of ham, spinach, sweet potatoes, bread and coffee. It was a very good dinner. Everybody is happy, thinking of going home soon. I helped to eat the bacon for two days rations, one and one-half pounds to each man with two pounds of hard bread, salt and pepper, and coffee with sugar. I packed my roll for stiff inspection for tomorrow. For supper we had cornwilly hash, prunes, bread and coffee. I received a letter from Norma. This ends my day's work and now it is 10:00 P.M. and time for me to go to bed.

9-5-1916 We got up at 4:30 P.M. for morning exercise. We policed the street. For breakfast mess we had beans, scrambled eggs, and beets. At 7:15 A.M. we left camp for inspection at the Aviation Field which was a distance of four miles away. It was a stiff inspection of rolls, rations, and rifles. We were reviewed for General Pershing. We had a very good line. The inspection took about five hours. Since we had no dinner, I ate a package of my hard bread and made some coffee. After our inspection, we marched to our Outpost for tonight. The weather is hot and somewhat cloudy. At about 9:30 P.M. there was a terrible thunder and lightning storm with a heavy downpour. The storm kept up steadily for one and one-half hours. The Rio Grande River flooded my tent. I went on post at 10:00 P.M. until 1:30 A.M.

9-6-1916 I got back to camp from the Outpost at 6:00 A.M. For mess we had meat, potatoes, hard bread and coffee. It was a very nice morning. I slept for two hours. Noon mess was beef stew, bread and tea. In the afternoon I was detailed to the Ordinance Department for tents. For retreat and the evening parade our Company had a very good line and was complimented from the Colonel. There were heavy winds blowing about mess time. We had cornwilly hash with ketchup, bread and coffee. Today we were placed in the mess hall by squad tables. Our squad started a profanity box today. Any man swearing at the table is fined ten cents per offense. This money goes towards helping to buy extras for our meals. It rained very hard for a few minutes with thunder and lightning – came up very suddenly. It is now 9:30 P.M. I waited for the mail, but there was none. Now for some sleep.

9-7-1916 For breakfast after morning exercise we had bacon, spuds and coffee. We policed the street. Morning drill was in battalion formation. It was a very interesting drill with Lieutenant Knight and Lieutenant Ingram in charge. Recall sounded at 11:30 A.M. For dinner we had meatballs, spuds, doughnuts and tea. We tried another system: one man in each squad goes up for the mess. Each day someone different has a turn. They think it can be done quicker this way. In the afternoon I was detailed at the Ordinances Department to help put up another tent. Later I helped take down the cook's tent and placed it in its proper place beside the kitchen. I took the water bag into another place. We had retreat and a parade with a perfect line in the review. We were complimented by the Major. After the parade we had our supper on account of refixing the cook shack. We had tomato sauce, bread, doughnuts, apricots and tea. One recruit came today at 8:00 P.M. Now for the bunk.

9-8-1916 Friday morning exercises and then mess of oatmeal, bread and coffee. We fell in for drill at 7:30 A.M. for a battalion drill – a good stiff one. It rained all morning. Noon mess was rice with stewed tomatoes which was burned, gingerbread, watermelon and tea. In the afternoon we were paid off. Evening mess was potato stew, bread, prunes and coffee. I didn't eat anything as I was not feeling well. Our Company goes on Guard Mount to-night. We started for the Bull Pen at 5:00 P.M. and arrived at 5:30 P.M. It's about three miles distance from the Camp. I am the sentinel on the number four box from 6:00 until 8:00 P.M., two hours on and four hours off. It was rather cool with some wind. I received a letter from Norma and a postal from Pratt.

9-9-1916 For morning mess we had shredded wheat, canned apples, prunes, a slice of bread and cocoa. I paid up all my debts leaving ten cents to spend ($1.00 to Red, $1.00 to Andrews, and $.25 to Crowley). Noon mess was beans, a pickle, bread and tea. I hiked from the Guard House to camp and arrived there at 7:45 P.M. for mess. We ate mess by candlelight with one candle on each end of the table. We had a good supper of frankfurts, sliced tomatoes, potatoes, bread, tapioca pudding and coffee. I received a letter from Norma.

The photos below show soldiers and desert plants and some local children with their burros and Walter in the middle photo with one of their burros.

9-10-1916 After Sunday morning exercises, at 6:00 A.M. we had mess of oatmeal, bread and coffee. At 9:00 A.M. we inspection of our feet. I wrote a letter to Norma and sent a card also. Then I had a bath. For noon dinner we had steak, mashed potatoes, bread, doughnuts and cocoa. In the afternoon we had to take down the tents for two hours to air them out. It was a pleasant afternoon with a little breeze. For supper we had cornwilly hash with potato, a pickle, bread, doughnuts and tea. During the evening parade, we had the best line in the review.

9-11-1916 We had morning exercises and then a breakfast of shredded wheat, bread and coffee. At 7:30 our Company fell in for drills in battalion formation until 11:30 A.M. For noon mess we had steak, potatoes, bread and cocoa. I was detailed to the lumber wagon in the afternoon. I didn't go on the parade this evening, but our Company had a splendid line. Evening mess was frankfurts, potatoes, pickles, bread and tea. I received a letter from Erhard and a bunch of blank post cards from the Norton Company. It is a nice moonlight night. I wrote to several people on the post cards.

9-12-1916 After morning exercises, we had drill call at 7:30 A.M. We drilled in battalion formation under Major Warren. Then we drilled one hour under the company commander in the skirmish exercises. We passed one and one-half hours in the Reserves for the firing line under Captain Burr of H Company. There were many criticisms and corrections in case of attack. We had oatmeal, bread and coffee for breakfast. Quite a few men were very sick from last night's mess. The frankfurts were awful and everybody had the runs. For noon dinner we had cornwilly "slop", bread and cocoa. In the afternoon I got into several pyramid pictures. I went to the mess hall and played the graphophone for a few minutes. It made me think of old times. I cleaned my rifle. The State Inspector inspected the Mass property. The weather was breezy. For evening mess we had cornwilly hash, pickles, bread and tea. During the evening parade, we had inspection of rifles. I received another letter from Norma and some bull from Grampa.

[A graphophone was an improved version of the phonograph. He mentions receiving "bull" here, and I think he meant bully beef, which was canned corned beef with the head of a bull depicted on the can.]

9-13-1916 We had Wednesday morning exercises and breakfast mess of oatmeal, cantaloupe, bread and coffee. After battalion drills under Captain Burr in extended order, our Regiment cleaned stones, etc. from the parade grounds. Noon mess was steak, potatoes, bread and coffee. In the afternoon I was detailed digging a ditch around the mess hall. When I finished with the detail, I wrote a letter to Norma. For evening mess at 4:00 P.M. we had corn stew, bread and tea. I rolled my pack and started for the Outpost about 5:20 P.M. for the evening.

Men lined up with shoulder bags (Walter is sixth from left)

9-14-1916 I returned from the Outpost about 6:20 A.M. For breakfast we had beans, bread and coffee. I went for a walk to get some caterpillars for Aldrich. On my way I picked what different flowers I ran into to press to look back into. I listened to the graphophone for a few minutes: "A Perfect Day" and "I Love You So" appealed to me the most. I dropped a card to Grampa to thank him for the "bull" he sent to me. For noon mess we had a slice of ham, turnips, cabbage, potato, bread and tea. It was quite windy this afternoon. We are getting ready for a hike to the range. Evening mess was cornwilly hash, bread and tea. We started for the range about 5:15 P.M. and arrived about 6:00 P.M. I was detailed to put up the officers' tent. It is a nice moonlight night, light enough to read a paper. I was full of the dickens tonight.

9-15-1916 We got up about 6:00 A.M. for morning mess of shredded wheat, cantaloupe, bread and coffee. The Company shot on a three hundred yard range in the morning. I got a score of thirty-six out of fifty ten shots. Noon mesh was "Goldfish", spuds, bread and coffee. I gave Eugene some money. We were marking targets all afternoon. For evening mess we had cornwilly hash, bread and cocoa. I didn't eat the hash. I went on a little hike around the mountains. On my way back I caught a small rattle snake about twelve inches long. I stepped on him before I saw or heard him. I skinned him as soon as I got back in camp. He had three rattles and one button.

[Goldfish loaf was made from salmon, bread crumbs, milk, eggs, and spices.]

9-16-1916 Saturday morning mess was oatmeal, bread and coffee. We shot by squad formation under Corporal Wilson at five hundred yards advancing to three hundred yards. I scored seventy-six hits. Our Company beat the record of ninety-six hits throughout the Regiment. After we got through shooting, Ranville and I went for a hike in the mountains. We saw many curious things on our hike. We returned to Camp about 12:30 P.M. and had our dinner of stew, potatoes, bread and coffee. We picked up empty shells on the skirmish work and returned to Camp at 4:00 P.M. At 5:15 P.M. we had our mess of beans, bread and coffee. After we finished eating, we started for the Outpost. We pitched our tents and I was put on first relief. We took a rifle from a civilian coming in from Mexico. We went on duty again from 1:00 A.M. to 3:00 A.M.

9-17-1916 About 6:15 A.M. we returned to Camp from the Outpost. We fell in for mess and were in line for a long time. We had steak, potatoes, bread and coffee. There was a big kick over the breakfast: the cooks got roasted by the Captain for the grub. We had inspection of our feet, etc. at 9:45 A.M. I shaved and cleaned up. After that, the mail came in and I received one letter from Miss Jacobson and the other from Flat. For noon mess we had ham, cabbage, potatoes, bread and lemonade. It was a pretty good dinner after the calling down. I cleaned my rifle. I'm pretty tired after being up last night. It's a very clear day with a little breeze. Our Company goes on Regimental Guard – I'm on first relief – rear guard on the Canteen. I went out at 5:00 P.M. For evening mess we had cornwilly hash, pickles, bread and tea.

The following photos are courtesy of Ellen (Asplund) Racine, curator of Northborough Historical Society. Taken by Clarence Nelson.

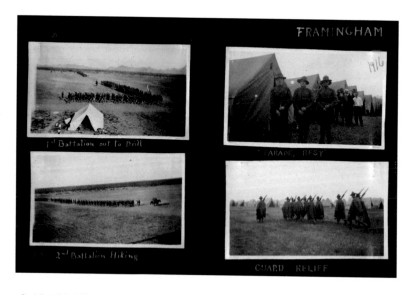

9-18-1916 I'm on Regimental Guard today. Morning mess was oatmeal, bread and coffee. We were ordered out to drill this morning on the parade grounds. I went on Guard from 11:00 A.M. to 1:00 P.M. at the Canteen. We had dinner mess at 1:15 P.M. consisting of hamburg steak, potatoes, peas, bread and cocoa. I sent postal cards to E.J., N.K., C.K., Mrs. K., W.F., and A. French.

It's a very pleasant day with breezes to keep us cooler. For evening mess we had one egg, bacon, potatoes, bread and tea. I was detailed as an orderly at Headquarters from 6:00 P.M. to 9:00 P.M. I did not feel very well when I went to bed – I had stomach cramps.

9-19-1916 Now it is three months since we were called to the colors. We had morning exercises, but I was too sick to keep up with the exercises. Sergeant Higgins ordered me to my quarters like a dog. I didn't have any breakfast today – for mess the men had shredded wheat. I reported to the hospital and they gave me a double dose of salts and some kind of a pill. For mess at noon they had beans and lemonade. I was very sick in bed all day. For evening mess they had corn stew and cocoa. I had toasted bread for two meals. I got a letter from Norma and a postal from Gramps. Taxes are due. It was 75th Anniversary Day. [I think the seventy-fifth anniversary is for his grandparents.]

9-20-1916 I got up for roll call and am marked for quarters today. For breakfast we had oatmeal, bread and coffee. I had only three pieces of toast and a little tea. Noon mess was steak, mashed spuds and lemonade. I laid in bed all day. For evening mess we had dried beef stewed with potatoes and tea. I had the same thing as I had at noon. I received a letter from Mrs. Remington. I played rummy with the boys in the evening. We had a minstrel show in camp last night but I could not go away from my quarters. It was a very pleasant day and rather cool in the evening.

9-21-1916 I went out to roll call, but didn't take part in the morning exercise. For mess they had oatmeal, bread and coffee. I had two pieces of toast and bought half a pint of milk. I am marked for my quarters again today. I answered sick call this morning. For noon mess the boys had a boiled dinner and lemonade. I had two pieces of toast with tea and no sugar. I played a bit of whist with the boys. The Company goes to the range to shoot today. It is a very pleasant evening. I stayed up until taps were blown. New orders came in tonight for calls – instead of getting up at 5:30 we get up at 5:55 A.M.

9-22-1916 I got up at 6:00 A.M. There were no morning exercises. Mess was at 6:30 A.M. – it was pancakes and coffee. I answered sick call again. I was marked ready for duty in the ranks. I had two eggs and toast with a cup of coffee. I was detailed to police the street. I was then detailed to clean and burn out the latrine. I did my week's washing. I cleaned up my tent. I wrote and mailed a letter to Norma. For noon mess we had ham, eggs, bread and cocoa. It was a very good dinner. I had the afternoon off. The new canteen opened this afternoon. I had a pint of ice cream, a box of graham crackers, and cracker jacks. The Company came back from the range at 5:45 P.M. For mess we had hamburg, spuds, bread and coffee. It was a fair supper. In the evening I played rummy with the bunch. I received a letter and a fountain pen from Norma.

Walter wrote the rest of his diary with that pen.

The following photo is of the canteen, church and post office taken by Clarence Nelson and provided by Ellen (Asplund) Racine of the Northborough Historical Society.

9-23-1916 Saturday morning mess was tomato soup, pears and coffee. I policed the street. We had inspection of the government property and laid on our cots in the streets. I was detailed to the commissary for food supplies. After inspection, we took down our tents. The wind and sand is blowing to "beat the band". Noon mess was beans, pickles, bread and cocoa. It was very windy all day. I shaved and cleaned up in the afternoon. I had a pint of ice cream and some cookies. We had retreat and a parade. We had a very good line in the review. We had our supper mess at 6:00 P.M. We had Goldfish, spuds and cocoa. I didn't eat the Goldfish – I couldn't touch it – it was too mushy.

9-24-1916 Sunday morning exercises were followed by morning mess of cornflakes, bread, a piece of cheese and cocoa. It was a nice breakfast. I policed the street and then took a shower and bath. I cleaned my rifle. At 12:00 P.M. I fell in for mess of roast beef, potatoes, peas, bread and cocoa. I didn't do much in the afternoon, but rolled my pack for Guard Mount tonight. We had an early supper at 4:00 P.M. on account of Guard Mount. For evening mess we had peaches, bread and butter, a piece of cake and tea. I received candy and cookies from Norma today. This was fine and came in good shape. I gave Bert Forsberg and Henry Frosh a treat. I was detailed as orderly for Base Headquarters until 10:00 P.M. I rode to camp on the post truck.

9-25-1916 I got up at reveille and went to mess at 6:00 A.M. I had eggs and toast with a piece of butter. I sent two packages to Norma in the morning. I walked from camp to town. I cleaned up for orderly duty. I had mess at the Bull Pen mess hall. We had a good boiled dinner. I reported for duty at 1:00 P.M. delivering messages. I was relieved after Guard Mount. Company B is going on Guard. I came back to Camp on a truck. I finished writing a letter to Norma and three postals to the Kjellbergs. I feel pretty tired. I will turn in tonight and I feel sure of a good sleep.

9-26-1916 After morning exercises we had mess of shredded wheat, canned cherries, crackers and coffee. I policed the street. Our Company fell in for drill at 8:00 A.M. We had close order drill for one hour. We had a school on advanced and rear guard work. A manual of arms finished the morning work on the field. Noon mess was steak, potatoes, bread, pie and cocoa. It was a good dinner. At 3:00 P.M. in the afternoon we had our fingerprints taken and any scars on our person was noted also. It took until time for retreat for about half the company. Then we had retreat and an evening parade after which we had our mess of macaroni and what they called stewed tomatoes. Hardly anyone ate it – it didn't seem to suit the boys. After mess there was some trouble in the street about the mess. The Company street was under guard to keep them in the street. I was one of the guards for one hour and 20 minutes. I received a card from Dave Chellberg from El Paso. I feel pretty disgusted tonight for special reasons.

[I think Walter, along with the other soldiers, was disgusted with the evening mess. However, he said "special reasons," which leads me to believe he was homesick and really missing his beloved Norma. I know family was especially important to him, and he did get depressed at times.]

9-27-1916 We had morning exercises followed by mess of oatmeal, bread and coffee. I policed the street. Morning drill was at 8:00 A.M. We had rear and advance guard work with battalion formation under Captain Burr of H Company, finishing with manual of arms for our morning's work on the field. I signed the payroll for State Pay in care of Norma. Noon mess was beans, pickles, bread and lemonade. It was a good dinner. The weather was very windy with sand blowing all around. The Regiment went out on the field in the afternoon to see an exhibition drill by Mounted Scouts. It was a very interesting drill given by them. I cleaned my rifle for inspection tonight. We had retreat and an evening parade. Mess was at 6:00 P.M. We had steak, burned spuds, apricots and tea. The Company was confined to the Company street, under guard.

9-28-1916 We had morning exercises and then mess of corn flakes, crackers, bread and coffee. I signed the Federal payroll. I policed the street. Morning drill was at 8:00 A.M. with the battalion drill under Captain Burr. The battalion was on advance work with our squad acting as the point. Major Foote's battalion acted as the enemy. It was very interesting work. Since it was very windy out there, the rising sand gave us away a little. We came in from the field at 11:30 A.M. and had noon mess of beef stew, corn-willy, pickles, bread and lemonade. It was a fair dinner. I wrote several letters and cards to friends today. I cleaned my rifle and bayonet for inspection. For retreat and the evening parade we had a good line in review. Evening mess was corn stew, bread and cocoa. We had a sociable game of whist. I sat with Sergeant Clark, Bennet, and Dirigon. I got beat 20 to 21 their favor. It's rather cold tonight.

9-29-1916 After morning exercises we had mess of oatmeal, bread and coffee. I policed the street. Morning drill was at 8:00 A.M. with battalion drill under Major Warren. Manual of arms was by Major Warren. We had Advance Guard work with Company C as the point. "A" Company was the main column. The Company drilled in close order work with manual of arms by the Company. Recall from the field finished the morning's work. We had a good noon mess of a boiled dinner, bread and lemonade. Five minutes after our dinner, we had good news – orders to go home. The whole Regiment all cheered and was glad to hear the news. We were all excited over the whole Regiment. I sent Norma a postal immediately after the orders for going home. I received a letter from Norma today. For evening mess we had flapjacks, bread and cocoa. I had Outpost tonight near the Aviation Field about three miles from Camp.

9-30-1916 I came back to Camp from the Outpost about 6:20 A.M. in time for morning mess of flapjacks and bread fried in eggs with coffee. I rolled my pack for muster and cleaned my rifle for inspection. Muster call was at 8:50 A.M. We got back off the field about 10:30 A.M. for an inspection etc. at 11:00 A.M. Noon dinner was beans, pickles, bread and cocoa. It was a good dinner. I received a postal card from Gramps. We took our tents down for airing out. I was on kitchen detail today. For evening mess we had cornwilly hash, spinach and tea. We had retreat and a parade at 5:00 A.M. We had a good line in review. I received a postal from Maurice Fitzgerald. Tonight we played a bit of whist. I won one and lost one.

10-1-1916 We had morning exercises and then mess of shredded wheat, cantaloupe and coffee. It was a good breakfast. I policed the street. I finished washing my clothes and took a bath. The Company got ready to go to the range. For dinner we had meat, mashed potatoes and cocoa at 11:00 A.M. At 11:45 A.M. we started for the range and arrived about forty minutes later. The shooting company made a very good score. I was detailed to count the hits made by our company. I killed a large tarantula that wandered up on the range. We started back from the range about 5:20 P.M. We had mess at 6:10 P.M. of Scout soup, bread and tea. It was a pretty good supper. After supper I cleaned my rifle. We had farewell services at the church tonight. We saw a flock of wild coyotes which didn't seem very afraid of us as we advanced on them. They just stood and looked at us.

Photo taken by Clarence Nelson, courtesy of Ellen (Asplund) Racine, Northborough Historical Society

10-2-1916 Following morning exercise, we had mess of oatmeal, bread, pears and coffee. I policed the street. At 8:00 A.M. morning drill was advanced guard work under Captain Doone of E Company. The last half of the morning A Company and C Company came unto H Company and E Company in a line of attack. E Company was fooled by us sending a flank out to keep them from getting a line on the main body. We returned from the field at 11:30 A.M. and fell in for State Pay amounting to $8.40. I paid $.85 to Whitney and $1.00 to Greenhalge. For noon mess we had hamburg steak, onions, potatoes, bread, pears and cocoa. It was a very good dinner. We are getting things ready for departure this afternoon. I paid up all my debts today out of the State Pay. I rolled my pack for the Outpost tonight. We had a hurricane in the rear which blew over some of the latrines. I started on my hike for the Outpost about 5:30 P.M. and arrived there about 6:00 P.M. I was on guard from 7:30 P.M. to 1:30 A.M. It was pretty cool all night. Evening mess was potatoes, beets and bacon.

10-3-1916 I came back from the Outpost at 6:00 A.M. and had morning mess of oatmeal, pears and coffee. We received Federal Pay at 7:30 A.M. I slept all morning. Noon mess was cornwilly stew, bread and "bum" coffee. Nothing very much happened in the afternoon. We had retreat and an evening parade. For supper we had tomato soup with hard bread and cocoa. I went to town tonight and bought a few necessaries. I also bought some bananas, oranges and apples for the morning's breakfast. I received a letter from Norma.

10-4-1916 After morning exercises we had mess of flapjacks, syrup and coffee. I also had a banana and an orange. It was a good breakfast. I policed the street. Morning drill was at 8:00 A.M. with battalion drill under Major Warren. The Company drill was in platoons. We had a school of instruction on out guard, deploying the same. This finishes the morning work on the field. Noon was a good meal of meat, potatoes, peas and cocoa. With this I had tomatoes, Mexican melon and oranges. I didn't do very much in the afternoon. We had retreat and a parade with a very good line in the review. We had inspection of rifles by Lieutenant Murray. This was Lieutenant Murray's first time out on the evening parade since he was detailed to truck train. Supper was Goldfish, tomatoes, prunes and tea. I stayed in the street tonight.

10-5-1916 Following morning exercise we had mess of oatmeal, bread and coffee. I policed the street. I was detailed on the grain wagon. I finished the detail at 12:00 P.M. and had mess of hamburg, tomatoes, mashed potato, bread and cocoa. For extras I bought one dozen of doughnuts for the squad table. I didn't do very much in the afternoon. We had retreat and an evening parade in platoon formation. Lieutenant Murray inspected our rifles. For supper we had musical fruit, prunes, bread and tea. Following a big sandstorm, we had rain – the first rain since we were on the new Campsite. I received a letter from Norma.

[I think "musical fruit" is a reference to baked beans.]

10-6-1916 Morning exercises were followed by mess of oatmeal, bread and coffee. I policed the street. At 8:00 A.M. we had drills and Regiment parades in platoon formation. We struck camp at 9:00 A.M. For noon mess we had beef pie, bread and cocoa. Evening mess was peaches and bread. We left the Camp at 10:00 P.M. We finally got settled in tourist pullman cars. We passed through New Mexico and Texas.

10-7-1916 Morning mess was beans, bread and coffee. I was sightseeing all the way. Noon mess was served at 4:00 P.M. It was bacon, cabbage, baked spuds and cocoa. I was put on guard in the vestibule for two hours. We passed through Oklahoma and Kansas.

10-8-1916 Morning mess was oatmeal, pears and coffee. Noon mess was ham, eggs, spuds and cocoa. For supper we had jam sandwiches with cocoa. I was on guard two hours tonight.

10-9-1916 Morning mess was beans, bread and coffee. Dinner was stew, potatoes and cocoa. We stopped at Kansas City, Missouri. Our Company had a walk around town.

10-10-1916 In Missouri we had a breakfast of oatmeal, bread and coffee. There was a big wreck delaying our passage. We stopped at a large brick mine in Randales, Missouri. It's very cold here. Andrews borrowed $1.00 from me. For dinner we had meat, spuds and cocoa. For supper we had crackers and bananas. We stopped in Springfield, Illinois for a while.

10-11-1916 For breakfast we had bacon, potatoes, and pears. We stayed in Chicago, Illinois for some time. Then we passed through Indiana into Ohio.

10-12-1916 In Kent, Ohio we had morning exercises. We passed through Pennsylvania.

Walter in New Jersey

10-13-1916 We stopped in Port Jervis, New York for exercises. The Company went through the town site seeing. We passed through New York.

10-14-1916 We passed through Connecticut and Rhode Island.

10-15-1916 We arrived in Massachusetts.

11-4-1916 We were mustered out of service.

The photo below is of Co. A, 2nd Mass Infantry taken by Clarence Nelson and provided by Ellen (Asplund) Racine of the Northborough Historical Society.

Chapter 3:

Walter Returns to Civilian Life

Walter returned to his home in Worcester, Massachusetts. On his enlistment papers his occupation was listed as student. However, I don't know if he returned home to attend college or obtained employment at Norton Abrasives Company where Norma worked. I suspect he did work at Norton Company, because he received so many letters from Norton Company employees while in France.

Norton Abrasive Company was started in the Greendale section of Worcester, Massachusetts, by John Jeppson and other Swedish immigrants from the Hoganas area of southwest Sweden. Norma's mother had also immigrated to Worcester from Hoganas.

Another possibility is that he may have begun a new job at U.S. Envelope at 75 Grove Street in Worcester, where he worked most of his life. One thing I know for sure is that he returned to his first and only love—Norma—and became engaged to her on July 19, 1917. Ironically, he was severely wounded a year later on July 20, 1918, at the Battle of Chateau Thierry in France. I believe his and Norma's prayers helped him through this difficult time of his life.

Chapter 4:

Walter Volunteered for Military Service in World War I

The photos below show the volunteer National Guard marching down Main Street in Worcester, probably in March when first mustered. The Levi Lincoln house is in the rear on the left. Levi Lincoln Jr. was the thirteenth governor of Massachusetts.

The above photo is on the corner of Main and Elm Streets, Worcester, Massachusetts

Although the United States endeavored to remain neutral in World War I, except for supporting Great Britain and other Allied Powers with much needed supplies, the United States entered WWI on April 6, 1917, after German submarines attacked U.S. merchant ships. Walter and his brother Eugene were called out for service in France on March 25, 1917. Walter had been in New Hampshire at the time and returned to Massachusetts, I believe, in Westfield, according to his diary.

According to Wikipedia, beginning in 1905 a summer training camp called Camp Bartlett in Westfield, Massachusetts, was used as a military training area for the Massachusetts Army National Guard. During August and September of 1917, Westfield was used as a staging area for training troops from Massachusetts and other New England states. Walter enlisted on September 10, 1914, in Worcester, Massachusetts. The military reformed the militia units of the Massachusetts National Guard and other New England National Guards into the 103rd and 104th infantry regiments of the 52nd infantry brigade in the 26th "Yankee" Division. They were transported to France on October 4, 1917, according to Walter's enlistment record.[2]

Walter and Eugene were in Company A in the 104th infantry regiment in the 52nd Brigade in the 26th Division in the American Expeditionary Forces (A.E.F.). Major General John J. Pershing commanded more than two million U.S. soldiers on battlefields in France. They left Massachusetts on October 4, 1917, and arrived on the Western Front in October of 1917. The United States built a strong military for this war. A cease fire was negotiated on November 11, 1918.

[The following is a direct account transcribed from Walter's diary concerning his service during World War I in late 1917 and 1918 in France. As his granddaughter, I felt that he was speaking directly to me in his diary. For instance, in many places he wrote: "Believe me…" Additionally, he wrote so much about his feelings although the "words" were usually in symbols.

Please note that he devised a system of symbols for the letters of the alphabet that he used for passwords, difficult things to talk about (such as "getting shelled" and "finding an entire trench of dead marines") and his feelings. I was able to figure out the letters of the alphabet for the symbols he used, because he later put the password under the symbols. This provided me with enough clues to decode his symbols.]

The above photos show the volunteer National Guard marching down Main Street in Worcester, Massachusetts, presumably to guard bridges and to train at Camp Barrett at Green Hill.

3-25-1917 Massachusetts National Guard called to arms.

[In Wikipedia it states that shortly after the United States declared war on Germany in April 1917, the 104th Infantry Regiment from Massachusetts and all other New England states were assigned to the 52nd Brigade of the 26th Yankee Division. All were volunteers.][3]

4-2-1917 Massachusetts National Guard left to guard bridges.

7-1-1917 Massachusetts National Guard called to Camp Barrett (at Green Hill in Worcester, MA).

7-25-1917 Mustered in N.S. Regular Army from the National Guard.

8-20-1917 MA National Guard left for Camp Bartlett in Westfield, MA.

The following photo was taken by Clarence Nelson of the soldiers on the trolley trip from Springfield. It is provided by Ellen (Asplund) Racine, curator of the Northborough Historical Society. Walter Krieger is the third soldier from the right.

10-4-1917 Massachusetts troops left Westfield, MA for France. We took the train through to Montreal, Canada.

10-5-1917 We took the transport ship S.S. Scotian to Halifax, Nova Scotia, where we waited to meet the other troops and then to travel to England.

Indian Harbor in Nova Scotia

Walter's grandson-in-law John Asplund holding his youngest son, Dana Richard Asplund (Walter's great-grandson), and Walter's second great-grandson, Kurt Walter Asplund, at Peggy's Cove near Halifax, Nova Scotia. Halifax Bay is in the background.

Walter's great grandsons at Peggy's Cove near Halifax, Nova Scotia.
Kurt Walter Asplund on left and Walter's oldest great-grandson, Erick Sanfrid Asplund

The following photo was taken by C.W. Robertson of machinery to be loaded on the ship in the background in the bay at Halifax, Nova Scotia. Provided courtesy of Ellen (Asplund) Racine, curator of Northborough Historical Society.

10-9-1917 We laid in the harbor from October 9th to 14th. I was very sick with a sore throat on the trip from Montreal to Halifax and went to the hospital. The weather was very clear with a little breeze. I left the hospital on October 13th. Part of the 102nd Regiment came into the harbor on October 13th. I am detailed as a life guard on the number two boat to prevent anybody rushing the boat in case of being torpedoed. It rained quite hard this afternoon.

10-14-1917 We left the harbor at 3:00 P.M. on October 14th with nine ships sailing in our convoy. Instead of taking a straight course to England, they are sailing in a zigzag course. I figured about seven minutes in each direction. The names of the ships sailing in the convoy are Scotian, Baltic, Justica, Magantic, Cherryleaf, Amazola, Pearleaf, Parkling and Karmaka. Captain Williams is in charge of the Scotian that I'm on. The ship does about fourteen knots during the day and about twelve knots at night. We had two hail storms at sea.

Ships in Halifax Harbor taken by C.W. Robertson provided by Ellen (Asplund) Racine, curator of Northborough Historical Society

10-18-1917 This evening we had a concert which was appreciated by all. It was mostly our own talent with some of the ship's crew. They did pull off some funny ones. A collection box was passed around for the benefit of the "Old Sailor's Home."

10-21-1917 We met the destroyers today.

[Wikipedia states that World War I destroyers were one thousand tons and larger with high speed and good heavy seas performance. They had fuller hulls and a flush deck with four smokestacks, which resulted in greater hull strength to better withstand torpedo attack. The destroyers had four four-inch fifty caliber guns and twelve twenty-one-inch torpedo tubes, as well as three twenty-three-caliber anti-aircraft guns. Anti-submarine armament was also included. They could travel at thirty-five knots, which is sixty-five kilometers an hour.][4]

10-23-1917 We landed in Liverpool, England on October 23, 1917 and left the boat on the morning of the 24th. I sent a letter to Norma when we arrived in Liverpool.

The following photo was taken by C.W. Robertson and made available by Ellen (Asplund) Racine of the Northborough Historical Society

10-24-1917 On Monday October 24th we boarded the steam Ry. L.N.W. Railway at 9:30 A.M. and arrived in South Hampton, England about 7:15 P.M. that night for a rest camp.

10-25-1917 We marched to the South Hampton common (in the rain), otherwise known at the soldiers' rest camp which was about two and one-half miles from the dock. It rains here almost every day; comes mostly from the bursting of shells upsetting the clouds. We bought cocoa at the Y.M.C.A. for one penny a cup. They have girls as conductors on the cars which costs one penny a ride. The tents we sleep in hold ten men cramped in very tightly.

The following photo of the train station in France was taken by C.W. Robertson and provided by Ellen (Asplund) Racine of the Northborough Historical Society

10-26-1917 I took a stroll through the suburb of Shirley and it was a very pleasant walk and very picturesque through there. The houses are very small and low, most of them are made of brick. I dropped another letter to Norma when I came back from my stroll. I bought another cup of cocoa at this time.

10-27-1917 I went down through the town of South Hampton tonight site seeing through bar rooms, etc. Girls instead of men serve the drinks. This didn't tempt me at all.

10-28-1917 We left South Hampton at 6:00 A.M. I was on detail to load the baggage on S.S. Archangel with H. Company and 600 horses with their remounts.

[The 26th was the first full division to arrive in France. The 104th Infantry consisted of Companies A (Light Infantry), C (City Guards), and H (Wellington Rifles), all from Worcester. The 102nd Field Artillery Batteries B and E were also from Worcester. Major General Clarence R. Edwards organized the Yankee Division and conducted the training, which made it the highest class combat division that it turned out to be. The training was conducted at Neufchateau. The Yankee Division approved a shoulder sleeve insignia with a "YD" monogram.][5]

10-29-1917 We arrived safely across the channel and docked at LeHavre, France. We were never so short of tobacco as we are nowadays. We left LeHavre at night in freight cars with thirty-six to forty men packed into them and believe me they were like sardines.

10-30-1917 We passed through the city of Rouen, France, a very large place, went through a tunnel that took almost twenty minutes to pass through. Next we passed through Bievres and Igny which has very good farming in these districts.

11-1-1917 We passed through Wissons, Orly, Limeil, and Mandres. We hiked from the train to the town of Sartes and it was quite a hike. We billeted here.

[Sartes is located in the township of Neufchateau, in the Vosges department, and Lorraine region in northeast France].

11-2-1917 I am detailed as Military Police in this place. The weather is very damp and muddy. We are about twenty-eight to thirty miles from the Front line trenches.

11-3-1917 I wrote my fifth letter to Norma today.

11-5-1917 I signed my payroll and wrote to Alice Reagan, Westfield, MA and Frenchy at the same time. We changed reliefs of Proval Guard and I am on from 2 to 6 A.M. We were issued steel helmets today.

11-8-1917 It's very muddy, wet and there's a cold wave today. I received a letter from Westfield and a box of chocolates from E.W. Aldrich. I sent Aldrich a letter thanking him for the chocolate.

11-10-1917 Saturday. It's rainy and very muddy. Sometimes the sun would shine, but very seldom. For breakfast we had a very good cornwilly stew mixed with onions, chips of bacon, three small biscuits and black coffee. At noon we had beans, a pickle, two pieces of bread and coffee. I shaved myself and took a sponge bath this afternoon. Then I sharpened a couple of razors, one for Hoby and one for McCabe. For supper we had spoonfuls of hamburg steak, a spoonful of mashed potatoes, two pieces of bread and black coffee.

11-11-1917 Sunday. For breakfast we had four small pieces of bacon, a spoonful of spuds, one piece of bread and black coffee. I sent Aldrich's the letter today. The weather was very cloudy and damp. For dinner we had beef stew, two pieces of bread and black coffee. In the afternoon it cleared up a bit with a little sunshine. We were expecting General Pershing, but he didn't come. We played a bit of whist and I lost by four points. I retired very early about 8:00 P.M.

11-12-1917 For breakfast we had cornwilly stew, syrup, three small biscuits and black coffee. It was a very good breakfast. The weather was fair but rather damp. I slept after breakfast. We had four pieces of bacon, spuds, three biscuits, syrup and black coffee. After dinner I wrote a letter to Norma #6. For supper we had loose hamburg, spuds, onions, two pieces of bread and black coffee. It had a very good taste. I retired at 8:00 P.M.

11-13-1917 Breakfast was "dish water", two pieces of bread and coffee. I received a card and two letters from Norma #5 and #6 from her. The weather was very clear and the sun was out and it's about time. The boys went in the Instruction trenches for the first time, being shown how to handle hand grenades and to fire the new rifles holding sixteen shots. They were gone all day and took rations with them consisting of cornwilly, onions and a hunk of bread. We had a fine supper of steak, onions, spuds, bread, biscuits and coffee. We were told we were to be paid tomorrow afternoon at 1:00 P.M. The trenches are made in a zigzag manner to help stop some of the shells. We had a letter stating that the Antilles was sunk while homeward bound with seventy lives lost. I retired early about 7:00 P.M.

11-14-1917 Pay call sounded this morning during reveille. For breakfast we had bacon, spuds, bread, syrup and coffee. It was a good breakfast. I cleaned and washed up this morning. For dinner we had cornwilly stew, with carrots, spuds, onions, bread and coffee. It was a very good mess. Right after we ate our dinner, we fell in for our pay. I got 308 francs. $15.00 was allotted for home. For supper we had good steak, one spud, three pieces of bread, syrup and coffee. It was a good supper. I'm retiring early as I am changing reliefs tomorrow from 6:00 to 10:00 A.M.

11-15-1917 For morning mess we had cornwilly, bread and coffee. It was very clear with the sun shining all day. Noon mess consisted of loose hamburg, spuds, bread and coffee. General Clarence Edwards came here today and gave us a talk on the situation and about discipline. He's a very interesting talker. He told about his experience on the Front. He was the one responsible for training us. For supper we had steak, spuds, bread, jam and coffee. I was relieved off the M.P. (Military Police) to report back to our Company. There was nothing much to do after supper but go back to bed.

11-16-1917 For breakfast we had bacon, spuds, bread, syrup and coffee. The Company will go out in the trenches for practicing machine gun work and also throwing hand grenades. I didn't fall in this morning but in the afternoon I did fall in and we dug trenches which was very hard to dig. It is mostly this thick, sticky clay and soft rock. It is very hard to dig in this kind of soil. Between relief we were out drilling. For dinner we had cornwilly stew, bread and coffee. For supper we had roast beef, spuds, bread and coffee. It was a very good supper. The day was a peach all through. I retired early as there was nothing to do.

11-17-1917 Morning mess was roast beef hash, spuds, syrup, bread and coffee. We had an inspection of quarters and our equipment. I got a pass to Neufchateau and had a swell time. We walked there and back again, making a twenty mile hike in all. Diriagan and I were together all the time. We went through the whole town. I bought several necessities that I needed. We started at 11:30 A.M. and arrived there at 12:45. We made swell time. When we got back to Sartes at 11:00 P.M., I was pretty tired. I don't think I will attempt another walk there again.

11-18-1917 No mess for me this morning, for I slept all morning. I got up at noon for mess which was cornwilly stew, bread and coffee. I went on guard duty at 5:00 P.M. and was on first relief. For supper we had roast beef hash, spuds, bread, syrup and coffee. I got to bed after I was relieved of guard duty which was at 10:30 P.M.

11-19-1917 I went on guard duty from 5:00 A.M. to 8:30 A.M. Breakfast was bacon, spuds, bread, syrup and coffee. For dinner we had loose hamburg, spuds, syrup, bread and coffee. In the afternoon I got two letters dated October 11th and 15th. I received all my mail up to date. For supper we had salmon, spuds, bread biscuits, and coffee.

11-20-1917 Breakfast was bacon, biscuits, bread and coffee. We drilled all morning in the trenches. We tried out the F.M. Gun (field machine gun) this morning. I had the position as first Preveyer. It was very interesting work throughout. We came back about 11:00 A.M. We have French soldiers as in-structors. Noon mess was tomato soup with rice, bread and coffee with milk (yeah!). In the afternoon we went out for company drill in approach formation for battle at the Front. We had Trapez and Lozenge shaped formations also. This is the way we had it thousand 1,1 1111. We returned from drill at 4:00 P.M. Retreat was at 4:30 P.M. For supper we had steak, spuds, biscuits, bread and coffee.

11-21-1917 Morning mess was cornwilly hash, bread and coffee. In the trenches with the F.M Gun, we had instructions precisely the same as yesterday only today it rained and was very muddy and wet. For dinner we had beef stew, bread, butter and coffee. We had the afternoon off to do necessities about the camp. I went to Sommerecourt today and didn't eat supper with the company. We were headed for Goncourt but decided to try it again since it rained so hard. I bought some chocolate and some crackers. The ninth Regulars are en-camped in Surrycourt.

The following photo is of Company A with Walter Krieger in the middle at the top and Eugene Krieger third from the left at the bottom.

11-22-1917 Mess in the morning was bacon, spuds, bread and coffee. Morning drill was in the trenches. We are improving very much. Noon mess was beef stew, bread and coffee. In the afternoon we had close order drill including bayonet drill. "A" Company goes on guard, last two platoons. We returned from drill at 3:30 P.M. recall. Retreat was at 4:30 P.M. It gets very dark at this time of day. For supper we had cornwilly hash, bread and coffee.

11-23-1917 I went sick today with a very bad cold in the chest and a sore back. I didn't get up for morning mess. I went to the hospital today. For dinner I had salmon, bread and coffee. I got a letter from Norma on the sick bed which was letter number 7. I also got three packages, one with cigars, another with candy and the other with chestnuts. This was very much appreciated, believe me. For supper we had beef stew, bread and coffee. I wrote Norma my #7 letter.

[This may have been trench fever, which was a type of influenza with fever, weakness, dizziness, headaches, and back and leg pain, often with a rash. It was spread by body lice.][6]

11-24-1917 For breakfast we had bacon, spuds, bread and coffee. I was in bed with a temperature of 99.7 degrees. For dinner we had steak, spuds, bread and coffee. For supper we had beans, biscuits with a piece of butter and coffee. Some hospital care? – believe me! No medication at all! My temperature went up to 101.4 degrees. I felt pretty sick.

11-25-1917 I was too sick to eat breakfast this morning. My temperature was 101.4 degrees. I was sent in the ambulance to Neufchateau. It was about 12:00 noon before I was in bed. I took quinine every hour for four hours. I sweated very much.

[During WWI, quinine was used for malaria. I don't know if that's what Walter was suffering from; he never said.]

11-26-1917 The first thing this morning they gave me a highball of Castor Oil. After this, I was given cough syrup once in three hours. The meals are fair here. I didn't sleep much all night, because I was coughing very much. I heard heavy firing at the Front through the stillness of the night.

[Castor oil was used for constipation and as an anti-inflammatory.]

11-27-1917 I had a bad coughing spell last night. Morning mess was bacon, bread and butter and coffee. I had a dose of cough syrup this morning. It snowed here this morning for the first time since we've been here.

11-28-1917 The weather is fair today. I am feeling somewhat better. They brought my clothes down from the check room, so now I can get up and exercise. I will try to finish the #7 letter I started to write to Norma yesterday. I can not mail this letter until I get back to my A Company.

11-29-1917 Thursday. Today is Thanksgiving Day, but it's not at all like last year. It was a sad day for me. We managed to get a "smell" of the turkey. I got a part of the wing, but that was all. The weather is fair today.

11-30-1917 Today is my birthday – I'm now 24 years old. I was thinking what I would have gotten on this day if I had been at home. The day seems very long in the sick bed.

12-1-1917 The weather was fair and cold. Some attendance here! There was no doctor in the Ward all day long. I didn't sleep very well.

12-2-1917 It rained very hard early this morning and then the beautiful sun came out to spend a few hours with us. It's a treat to have the sun with us. A week ago today I came to this "wonderful" hospital.

12-3-1917 Although I was discharged from this hospital, I was not well when I left it. I arrived back in Sartes about 10:00 A.M. I lost my voice and can only whisper. I can not eat much of anything. I didn't sleep any last night until about 3:00 A.M.

12-4-1917 For morning mess I drank a cup of coffee – that's all. I was put on Jo Jo guard today. I am not feeling any better. I ate a little better today. The weather is very raw and at noon the sun shone a little. I was put in Captain Parker's quarters until he comes back from the trenches.

12-5-1917 I was sent to the hospital as an orderly to relieve Marvin until I get better. I am down with a bad attack of bronchitis and a cold.

12-6-1917 I can not eat much – I have no appetite at all. I wrote my #8 letter to Norma, one to Frenchy and one to Mrs. E.J. Thron. I received #9 letter from Norma. I also got a letter from French (which I answered).

12-7-1917 Nothing much doing today, but am still suffering from bronchitis.

12-8-1917 I am still at the hospital, keeping the fires going. I am not any better. The dear old folks I am living with are very kind to me.

[He is referring to Monsieur and Madame Champagne, who befriended him at the hospital and visited him often throughout his time in France. It sounded like they lived there at the hospital. They became very friendly with Walter and visited him often. I remember how my grandfather had a lot of friends; people were drawn to him. I also remember that my mother Evelyn had the same friendly, pleasing personality as her father.]

12-9-1917 It's a beautiful day – sunny and warm. I am still in the hospital as an orderly for the hospital janitor. The old folks gave us a rabbit supper in the evening and before going to bed Madame Champagne gave me some hot tea for my cold.

12-10-1917 It's very raw out today. At about noon time it got warmer but it's very muddy – something terrible. There are lots of funny things happening at the hospital every day. Madame Champagne is still giving me tea before going to bed.

12-11-1917 The weather is very windy and raw today. I am still an orderly at the hospital, but am not in love with the job. The old folks are taking better care of me than they did at the hospital when I was here before. We go to bed about 8:00 P.M. with the chickens.

12-12-1917 There's no sun today – it's rather cloudy and damp. A fellow detailed at the hospital gave us a few selections on his violin. Amongst the

songs he played "Sunshine of Your Smile, "Perfect Day" and "Auf Wieder-
sehen" etc. It was beautiful music. I was discharged from hospital duty this
morning and Private Roy Bates relieved me. He has been sick with the same
thing. I am not any better, but am back with A Company again. A company of
French soldiers passed through Sartes this afternoon. We are in the Vosges
section. I received another letter from Norma #11. I also received one from
Westfield, Massachusetts.

12-13-1917 Mess in the morning was rice, syrup, bread and coffee. A Company is on guard and detail work. I was detailed to the commissary chopping
wood, a very pleasant job. I finished at 3:50 P.M. I retired early about 8:00 P.M.

12-14-1917 Morning mess was rice, syrup, bread and coffee. We went up
to the trenches for instruction on F.MG. Fired Automatic weapons. It was very
foggy today, almost a rain. We came back at 10:00 A.M. Noon mess was loose
hamburg, spuds, bread and coffee. In the afternoon we had a school in the
Y.M.C.A. on the Automatic Rifle, parts etc. given by Lieutenant Howard. Madame Champagne made us some very nice waffles which tasted very good. I
retired about 9:00 P.M. I had a bad coughing spell all night.

12-15-1917 Mess in the morning was stew, bread and coffee. We had an
inspection this morning which I passed O.K. Lieutenant Robart inspected the
platoon. Noon mess was stew again. In the afternoon we had drill but I didn't
go out as I was pretty sick. I retired early about 8:00 P.M.

12-16-1917 Morning mess was rice, syrup and coffee. I didn't eat any
breakfast, as I wasn't hungry. I answered sick call and was marked for light duty
and am pretty well shot these days – my voice is very weak. Noon dinner was
beef stew, three biscuits, and coffee. During the afternoon, I wrote to Norma,
had a haircut and a shave. I spent the evening with the old folks. They had a
chicken supper for us. The French have a strange custom for serving food
where they serve the vegetables either before or after the rest of the meal. We
had cauliflower with the chicken pie (with the cauliflower served last). I bought
some dates to finish the supper. I enjoyed the dinner very much. After this,
we sat around the fireside discussing one thing or the other. My partner speaks
French which made things run smoothly. To end the evening Madame Champagne made my tea and I said, "Bon Soir" and retired for the evening.

[*Bon Soir* means good night.]

12-17-1917 Morning mess was rice, syrup, prunes, biscuits and coffee. Because I was marked for light duty, I was detailed to the commissary. Noon mess was stew, bread and coffee. I bought a pair of slippers for five francs. It snowed today but came down very slowly. I wrote my #9 letter to Norma. For supper mess we had steak, spuds, bread and coffee. After supper, I went up and got my chest rubbed. Then I went back to my billet and sat around the fireplace until it was time for bed. Madame Champagne went to bed early so Monsieur Champagne made my tea.

12-18-1917 Morning mess was bacon and mashed spuds, bread and coffee. I was marked for light duty again. Noon mess was beef stew, biscuits and coffee. I slept in the afternoon. For supper we had stew, biscuits and coffee. In the evening we had an apple pie made for us by Madame Champagne along with a box of dates. It tasted very nice. I had my tea and went to bed.

12-19-1917 Morning mess was rice, bacon, biscuits and coffee. I reported to sick call and was marked for light duty. I went to the commissary and drawed rates. After that, I had to go out and drill which was quite out of the ordinary for light duty. Noon mess served at 11:15 A.M. was hamburg stew, bread, one biscuit and coffee. We went to "Harrieville Hill". We had French open warfare work. It was very interesting work, although I was pretty sick at times. We came back from there at 4:00 P.M. Supper was beans, bread and coffee. I came back from supper and changed my stockings as they were pretty wet. I wrote a letter to Clara Lehmann to thank her for a box of sorted tobaccos which she had sent me. I was very surprised to get it. I saw Colonel Hayes for the first time since I landed here in France. I drank my tea and retired.

12-20-1917 Morning mess was bacon, spuds and coffee. I answered sick call and am back in the hospital again. For dinner I had two pieces of toasted bread and coffee. Nothing important happened this afternoon. For supper I had loose hamburg, spuds, bread and coffee. I tried hard to sleep but coughing prevented it quite a lot.

12-21-1917 For morning mess I had toasted bread and coffee. Several packages have come, but they are not going to give them to us until Christmas. I passed the morning quite comfortably. Noon mess was beef stew, bread and coffee. I spent the afternoon comfortably. A lot of mail came in today, but as yet there was none for me. Supper was rice and tomato stew, bread and some nicely made cocoa. Nothing more of importance happened.

12-22-1917 For morning mess I had bacon, spuds and bread. I was examined this morning. I am resting comfortably now. Noon mess was rice with hamburg and tomato stew, bread and coffee. I passed the afternoon pretty fair. Supper was beans, bread and coffee. In the evening two letters #10 and #12 and a post card from Norma dear arrived. I have received them all to date. Suipture came up to see me this evening and brought some dates with him. Madame Champagne sent me some apples and pears. While I was reading Norma's letter, Pheny was playing the violin. I think he did it to get my goat. He certainly can fiddle. The evening was a blessing and Norma's letters cheered me up a bit.

12-23-1917 Morning mess was oatmeal, bread and coffee. Bates won a box of cigars this morning and passed them around. Noon mess was stew, bread and coffee. The weather was fine with the sun out in the afternoon. Supper was mashed potatoes, bread pudding and coffee. It was a very good supper. Madame Champagne sent me some nice waffles which were fine tasting. She is very good to me. I am getting better, but my voice is no better. I will be glad to get out of bed for it is so tiresome! There were two French soldiers visiting us in the hospital. We gave them some smokes and they were glad to get them. They get only one which is not very much. The French are very sociable. Both of them had seen actual fighting. The troops got paid yesterday, but I have not received mine yet as I am in the hospital.

12-24-1917 Morning mess was rice, syrup, bread and coffee. Morning was passed comfortably. Noon mess was cabbage, stew, bread and coffee. Nothing much happened in the afternoon. Supper was loose hamburg, spuds, bread and coffee. It's the night before Christmas – such a difference from last year. Bates slept with me tonight. It was kind of tight, but we kept warm. There was quite a racket around the hospital tonight.

12-25-1917 Tuesday. Christmas Day. Morning mess was bacon, spuds and coffee. I received a Christmas present from Aunt Hedwig. Nothing else came for me. Noon dinner will not be until 2:00 P.M. this afternoon. Dinner consisted of turkey, carrots, spuds, bread pudding, coffee and nuts. It was a splendid feed. There was no supper for the dinner was served so late. "A" Company had their Christmas tree in the Y.M.C.A. They had some entertainment also. They say it came off fine. After the entertainment, the Christmas boxes from home were given out. On this day I got my #14 letter from Norma which pleased me so much! There was a package for me, but it was so late that they didn't bring it up. I slept comfortably but kept thinking of Norma. They say I talked in my sleep.

12-26-1917 Morning mess was oatmeal with Karo, bread, pudding and coffee. I got up from the sick bed and am feeling much better. I got the other letter #13 from Norma this afternoon, very pleasing to be sure. Along with this letter two letters came from Westfield and the Reagans. Noon mess was beef stew, bread and coffee. I didn't eat anything, as I was so excited over my mail. I am starting my #10 letter to Norma, but I don't know what to write about. Supper was rice stew with tomatoes, bread and coffee. In the evening they came up with a big box from Norma – some box, believe me! Everything was O.K. This was the first box. The photo of Norma was in it - I was crying for Norma. God bless my girl. Roy Bates slept with me last night.

12-27-1917 Morning mess was bacon, spuds, bread and coffee. I spent the morning writing to Frenchy, Pop Kjellberg, Aldrich, Pratt, the Throns, and Norton Company. Noon mess was beef stew, bread and coffee. During the afternoon, I rested. Supper was rice with prunes, bread and coffee. I passed the evening reading the magazines that Norma had sent me.

12-28-1917 Mess in the morning was oatmeal, bread and coffee. I wrote to father today, thanking him for the cigars he had sent me. It's Eugene's birthday today. Noon mess was a fine beef stew with bread and coffee. I spent the afternoon reading and sleeping. For supper we had tomato stew, bread and coffee. I received a toilet kit from Arthur Pratt. Lieutenant Corkum came up to see me in the hospital.

12-29-1917 Morning mess was bacon, spuds, bread and coffee. I was discharged from the hospital today. Noon mess was beef steak, spuds, bread and coffee. I ate my dinner with the Champagnes today. There is a lot of snow here. The weather is very bitter with a sharp wind blowing. Supper was beans, bread and coffee which tasted very good. I had a bath in the evening and went to bed about 8:00 P.M.

12-30-1917 Morning mess was toasted bread, a piece of pie and a cup of tea. We had an inspection this morning at 10:30. Dinner was beef stew, bread and coffee. We had a short range gun inspection this morning in the main street which was quite a surprise to all the men. I spent the afternoon in misery, discouraged and everything imaginable. The weather was fine with the sun shining. It was a glorious day, but there was nowhere to go. For supper we had loose hamburg, spuds, bread, bread pudding and coffee – a fairly good supper. Captain Parker returns today, so I was moved out of his quarters to number three billet with Lieutenant Murray's quarters. He is away to a gas mask school. As soon as he returns, I will be somewhere else.

12-31-1917 Morning mess was bacon, spuds, bread and coffee. We drilled this morning in combat formation and extended order work. We mustered for pay this morning at 11:30. Dinner was beef stew with vegetables, bread and coffee. At 1:30 P.M. during the afternoon, we had a drill doing rifle exercises. It was pretty cold up on the hill. We returned at 3:15 P.M. and had retreat at 4:10 P.M. For mess we had rice and tomato stew, bread and coffee. I went to bed at 8:00 P.M.

1-1-1918 New Year's Day. Two years ago at 12:00 P.M I started to go with my Norma. After breakfast of rice, syrup, bread and coffee, I went back to bed and slept all morning. We had a very good dinner of steak, mashed spuds, bread, pie and cocoa. Today they gave us a holiday as it was New Year's Day. It was a pleasant, sunny day all day. I rested in the afternoon until retreat at 4:10 P.M. For supper we had hamburg stew, bread and coffee. Then I went to wish the Champagnes a Happy New Year.

1-2-1918 Reveille was at 8:20 A.M. Morning mess was bacon, rice, bread and coffee. We had quite a strenuous hike this morning and then had open warfare maneuvers. It was very interesting, especially playing the part of barrage fire. We came back from drill about 11:30. For dinner we had beef stew, bread and coffee. For the afternoon drill at 1:20 we went to the same place with the same maneuvers as this morning, only we had two maneuvers with four Companies like this morning. We got back quite late. Retreat was at 4:10 P.M. For supper we had beef, mashed spuds, bread and coffee. I feel pretty tired tonight.

1-3-1918 Morning mess was bacon, spuds, bread and coffee. I was detailed to the commissary to draw rations for the cook shack. After we finished this detail, we went out and drilled close order and extended order. After dinner of loose hamburg, spuds, bread and coffee, we fell in at 1:20 P.M. and the company went up on the hill. We had bayonet exercises. I returned at 3:30 P.M. and had beef stew, bread and coffee for supper – the best I've tasted in a long time. I went to see Bates in the hospital. I feel pretty tired and am retiring early tonight.

1-4-1918 I spent two weeks and four days in all at the hospital, but haven't lost very much. We went up "Harrieville Hill" and had wave formation by battalion. It was very cold here today, we suffered pretty much with those dam shoes. My feet were very nearly frozen. Quite a sight to see a whole battalion at maneuvers. Recall was at 12:00. We fell in for afternoon drill at 1:30 P.M. We went to the hill again with precisely the same thing. Retreat was at 4:40 P.M. When we came back, we came through Pomperrie back into Sartes. I spent the evening in the billet as I was very tired. Retired very early.

[A billet was quarters in a private home.]

Walter's sketch below shows the formation of the platoon in combat form.

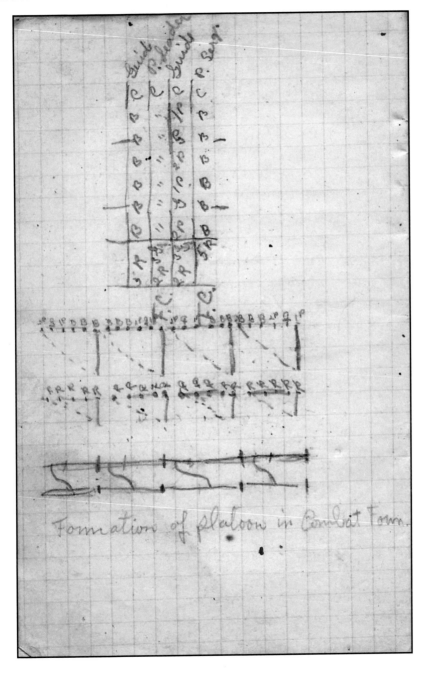

1-5-1918 Inspection of equipment was at 8:30 A.M. We fell in for mess at 10:30 A.M. Regimental maneuvers were from 11:30. We had quite some problems and lots of work. Marges, Corporal Rennet, Gillooly and myself were captured after climbing a steep hill of about 60 degrees. We were acting as flankers. The regiment returned to Sartes at 3:15. Retreat was at 4:40 P.M. I went up and delivered a letter to Bates at the hospital. I received a letter from my girlie #15. I went to bed early.

1-6-1918 Sunday. Reveille was at 7:00 A.M. I changed my bunk over to no. 23 Billet as Lieutenant Murray is expected today. I have a fine place. I worked all morning fixing my bunk. We had a very good dinner of beef stew, bread, pudding, coffee with milk. I came back and wrote #11 letter to Norma. Following supper mess, I wrote to the State House and father. It's raining here tonight - very funny weather with a warm wave blowing. The day was a peach with the sun out all day. I retired about 9:00 P.M.

1-7-1918 Reveille was at 6:30 A.M . It rained very hard, but that didn't prevent us from drilling. We had advance guard work and came back soaked. After we got back, we had details cleaning up the streets. Noon mess was terrible: "dishwater" bread and unsweetened coffee. This afternoon we fell in for a lecture by the Captain and Lieutenant Robart on military courtesy and discipline. It rained all afternoon. There was no retreat tonight, the first one that was postponed that I know of. My feet are swelled up, a result of being frozen. I never had any trouble like this before with my feet. It's raining to beat the cars. It's 7:00 P.M. and I'm retiring.

1-8-1918 Reveille was at 6:30 A.M. There was no drill, so we cleaned and oiled our rifles. This morning I shaved myself on the fly. At 10:00 we fell in and had advance guard work, marched towards Pomperrie and returned at 11:30. Fell in at 1:20 and first we had instructions on gas attack with our gas masks. These masks should take only six seconds to put on. After this, we had precisely the same march as this morning, only the battalion moved toward Somericourt. I was pretty tired and had freezing, wet feet. It snowed continuously all day long. I retired early this evening. Wine seems to be about the only thing we can drink, as the water is very poor and unsafe.

1-9-1918 At 8:20 we fell in for morning drills and hiked for about ¾ of an hour. Then we had bayonet exercises and marched back on a stiff hike until we came into Pomperrie. We rested there for fifteen minutes and then the company marched back to Sartes. At 1:20 we fell in and had close order drill in the streets. We then marched up to the mess hall and had instructions on the gas attack. Gas attack is a very important part of this game. We tried out getting them on in the quickest possible time. The captain gave us a lecture on feet and the care of them. We then went out and drilled close order until retreat at 4:20. Supper consisted of beans, bread and coffee We had seconds tonight. I felt very tired tonight, so retired early.

1-10-1918 Morning work was with the battalion. It was advance guard work, and we marched towards Soulacourt. In the afternoon we fell in with both gas masks and went up to the mess hall for more instructions on the gas masks. After supper, I went to see Madame Champagne. She was very glad to see me. I returned and retired early after my bath.

[The conditions on the Western Front in WWI were very difficult. A battalion consisted of three companies with about three hundred or four hundred soldiers in each one. Two companies would be stationed in the front trenches and the third would be several hundred yards to the rear. The front most companies would be in the trenches for twenty days to two weeks and the rear would be there five to seven days. There was no sanitation in the trenches; buckets were used for toilets. In the rear there were primitive latrines. The soldiers took "sponge baths" with wash cloths. When the battalion was pulled off the front lines, they were usually near a town three to five miles in the rear. Once there, they could get a shower. This was usually for two to three weeks.][7]

1-11-1918 Morning work was advance guard through sloppy snow and rain; very disagreeable weather today. It was a hard morning's work. The 103rd M.G. Company left this morning. After noon mess of beef stew, bread and coffee, the Company moved to the barracks. We worked all afternoon moving there. This makes my seventh time moving so far. After supper of loose hamburg, bread and coffee, I came back to my bunk and fixed things up to suit myself. After washing and shaving, I retired early.

1-12-1918 Saturday. We had the regular Saturday morning inspection of equipment. We also had venereal inspection and feet inspection. The weather is very good today with the sun shining and very clear. The Company fell in, had manual of arms and a hike. I didn't fall in, because I did not have any shoes to wear. I had a big head this afternoon, so I didn't eat supper tonight. I slept all the way through until morning.

1-13-1918 I rested this morning. We turned in what surplus stuff we didn't need. We had a very good dinner of steak, mashed spuds, bread, bread pudding and coffee. I wrote my #12 letter to my Norma and sent her a franc for a souvenir. The weather was fair today, a little snow and a little sun.

1-14-1918 I didn't get sent to drill this morning, because I didn't have any shoes that fit properly to wear. I stayed in the barracks and read the book Training for the Trenshiga, a very interesting book. I received a new pair of shoes tonight. I'm making preparation for tomorrow's problem: oiled my shoes. I have started to read the Bible tonight. I started from the first of the book. I will try to read a little each night before I retire.

1-15-1918 Morning mess was rice, syrup, bread and coffee. We started on the hike about 10:45 A.M. It was raining so that we were soaked to the skin by the time we got to the line trenches. The lines were filled with water. We had to wade through it just the same. This is the worst hike I have ever been on. The roads were very slippery which made it very hard to walk. On the hike we had eight ounces of hard tack – our soup kitchen broke down. The problem was supposed to last until midnight, but we were soaked and cold so they called it off. We returned to Sartes about 7:15 P.M. some eight miles march. I was all in and very tired; therefore, I didn't go to mess which was at 8:00 P.M. I retired at 8:00 P.M. and slept like a log.

[Sartes is in the Lorraine region of northeast France about 254 kilometers from Paris.]

1-16-1918 There was no reveille this morning. I got up about 10:00. We had inspection of rifles at 11:30 A.M. In the afternoon we had a lecture about the trench problem, duties there etc. After this we had gas mask instructions. It rained all afternoon. It was very muddy and wet, but there is no snow on the ground. There was a very warm wave blowing from the south. I cleaned my rifle thoroughly and then shaved and cleaned myself. We were paid today. I received two months' pay in all, 216 francs this month.

1-17-1918 I didn't drill today, for I couldn't get into my shoes. The company had maneuvers. I spent the afternoon reading. Something very interesting happened this afternoon. A French aviator was flying all around the village in his plane; he did many different stunts. The reason for his being here was that the propeller on his plane was worn and he had to try out his new one. He had to do these stunts before he proceeded on his journey. The airplane engine had 150 horse power with 9 cylinders. It was very cloudy and raining, so it was very muddy too. I'm feeling blue for Norma dear.

1-18-1918 We had reveille at 5:30. I was detailed to the commissary all day. We had a very light lunch of biscuits and coffee. There were Brigade maneuvers today and the Company took rations with them. The Company moved out at 7:15 A.M. and returned at 5:00 P.M. I finished my detail at 3 P.M. The weather was warm in the morning, but in the afternoon it got colder. I bought a pair of slippers which cost me eight francs and a towel which cost me three francs. I retired early about 9:00 P.M.

1-19-1918 Reveille was at 6:30 A.M. I shaved and cleaned up for inspection at 9:30 A.M. which was over at 10:30 A.M. In the afternoon the Company fell in for some details. After supper, the Company fell in for a hike to the trenches at 5:15 P.M. They will stay there until relieved by the 3rd Battalion which will probably be at 11:30 P.M. It was a beautiful night with the moon shining. Starting tomorrow, I am on permanent detail at the commissary.

1-20-1918 The boys came back from the trenches about 2:45 A.M. They felt pretty tired when they came back. Mess of stew, biscuits and coffee was about 11:00. I worked all morning at the commissary and didn't do much in the afternoon, but helped to unload bread from the wagon. We had only two messes today: supper was hamburg, bread, bread pudding and coffee. The day was a peach, but there was a heavy wind blowing. I felt pretty lonesome tonight for Norma. God bless her. I had a pleasant dream last night about Norma. I dreamed of a happy future. A man can endure just about anything if he has hope of things getting better. The men who were troubled with their feet were shipped away to a foot specialist. Quite a number went. I swore off of gambling. There was nothing much to do but to go to bed.

[Reading this diary, especially his comment above, made me realize how much Walter cared for Norma. I think that's what kept him going under such difficult circumstances.]

1-21-1918 I got up at 7:30 A.M. and reported for duty to the commissary at 8:00. I didn't eat any breakfast. I gave out supplies to the different Companies. In the afternoon our new Colonel Shelton gave us a few points on modern warfare. This was his first speech before us. He is from the regular army. He told us we were the first complete regiment, 3500 strong, to put foot in France. He is proud of his regiment. He also said if there was any fighting, we would be the first to be called upon. I received two loving letters from my girl tonight, the16th and 17th. Oh, how I felt when I read those letters. Now for bed.

1-22-1918 I reported to the commissary at 8:00 and went to Harrieville for commissary supplies. This was the first time I had been to this town since I stepped off of the train. I went over on the mule team from here. I came back at 12:00 and didn't eat anything but some toasted bread with butter and a cup of coffee. I made the second trip this afternoon and returned with a bag of first class mail and supplies. I received letter #18 from my girl. I must write by all means, or at least start it, but am very fatigued tonight. Now for my letter to Norma. I am looking straight at my girlie now, thanking her for writing to me. I finished writing letter #13 (ten pages) to Norma.

1-23-1918 I reported to the commissary at 7:45 and worked very hard all morning. I worked hard in the afternoon as well, until 3:00 doing odd jobs now and then. Colonel Brown made an inspection of our stores today. He is 63 years old and claimed to be the oldest officer in the service over here. After dinner, I went back to the commissary and unloaded two loads of supplies. After I came back to my bunk, I wrote a letter to Helen L. Sawyer and one to Maurice Fitzgerald. I felt very tired tonight.

1-24-1918 After reporting to the commissary at 7:45, I did not eat any breakfast, but worked pretty steadily all morning. Mess at noon was cornwilly, bread and coffee which was very good for a change. I didn't do very much, only a few odd jobs, this afternoon. There was an issue of smokes today from

"To Our Boys in France Tobacco Fund." For supper we had cornwilly stew with spuds, bread and coffee. I finished with some biscuits that I bought while in town. After returning to the commissary following dinner, I worked with the unload team. I got a pair of shoes tonight size 10EE. I left there at 7:00 and had a sick headache tonight. Therefore, I retired early.

1-25-1918 Reveille was at 6:00 today. I didn't eat breakfast this morning but slept until 7:30 and reported to the commissary for duty. The battalion went to the trenches today, taking with them one ration. They will return some time this afternoon. These trenches are about eleven kilometers from here. I received a box from Westfield, MA containing one fruit cake which was very good, three soaps, and one towel. We had a very good steak supper with spuds, carrots, bread and coffee.. I went back to the Commissary but didn't do much. I will hit the hay early tonight.

1-26-1918 I got up at 7:30 and reported to the Commissary, working all morning giving out rations. The weather was very foggy in the morning, but cleared up at noon with the sun at its best. The battalion was all on detail this morning, cleaning up around the town. They are going towards Harrieville this afternoon. There was a regimental review by the Colonel this afternoon. One team came in this afternoon and they did little odd jobs. After supper, we unloaded another team and then I went back to my bunk.

1-27-1918 After reporting to the Commissary at 7:45, I worked all morning furnishing supplies to the companies. I wrote a letter to my girlie, this making my #14. We had a very good supper of beef, turnips, mashed spuds 3 biscuits and coffee. I came back to my bunk and wrote a letter to Ma Kjellberg. I received a letter from Norma #19. The weather was very foggy and raw today. I will retire early tonight.

1-28-1918 I didn't eat any breakfast, but reported the Commissary at 7:45 and worked hard all morning and all afternoon. The weather was very good with the sun out. I received two letters from Norma #20 and #21 as well as a box of sweets. I also received a letter from Frenchy and one from Westfield, Mass. I feel very tired today and will retire early tonight.

1-29-1918 I reported to the Commissary at 7:45 and worked all morning. The weather was very pleasant, just like a summer's day. Bert Whitaker is on detail with me today. I had a piece of Ma's fruit cake which tasted very good. A pile of mail came in today, three boxes for me: two from Norma and one from Clara Lehmann. A fellow hasn't much time for himself nowadays. Up to now Norma has got seven letters on me. I looked over my boxes and they pleased me very much. I tried out the pipe Mr. Kjellberg sent me and was very much pleased with it.

1-30-1918 I reported to the Commissary at 7:45 and worked all morning. Sergeant Clason went to the gas chambers for the first time this afternoon. I was left alone at the Commissary. The sun was out this morning and it was very pleasant, but a very heavy fog swept over here so dense that you couldn't see. Such a fog! Everything is white with frost. I am writing my #15 letter to Norma tonight.

1-31-1918 Again I reported to the Commissary at 7:45 and worked all morning. Sergeant Clason goes to Neufchateau today. There was lots of work today. The battalion went to the trenches today. Since I was here alone, I ate dinner with C Company today. They had gulash, bread and coffee which was very good. Today, I noticed how pretty the trees and bushes looked, covered with white frost. They have been that way for three days. The frosty trees and bushes against the green grass was a sight that is very rare. There was a little fog today. I wrote to Mrs. Reagan today, thanking her for the boxes she sent me. Now I will retire.

[Walter was an artist and, I believe, painted that picture he just described years later with his pastels.]

2-1-1918 I reported to the Commissary at 7:45 today. We loaded rations and supplies. It has been three lonely months since we've been in this town. We could hear the noise of shells last night. It was foggy and raw. I came back to my bunk and made my bed. Then I wrote to Clara Lehmann and Frenchy tonight.

2-2-1918 It is very frosty and raw this morning. I reported to the Commissary at 7:45 and worked all morning loading salvage and supplies to the cook's shacks. I had a toot this morning after I got through cleaning out the basement to the Commissary. We are making preparations for moving out of this place. The sun was shining this morning in all its glory, a pretty sight to see the sun shining on the frosted trees and bushes. This afternoon was like a summer day. The regiment is having maneuvers this afternoon. This afternoon I shaved and cleaned up. I made some billy tea that Norma sent me which was very fine. It is a wild evening, believe me, it's 11:30 now. The boys are all raising a rough house!

[I think "billy tea" was a strong Australian tea cooked in a can or tin or kettle over a fire.]

2-3-1918 I reported to the Commissary at 7:45 and worked hard all morning. I was put in charge while Sergeant Clason went to Harrieville. The weather was very clear and the sun was out like a summer's day. I stayed at the Commissary until 3:00. I came back to my bunk and wrote to Norma, my #16 letter. I mentioned in it a change in my allotments, getting things ready for the trip. At 5:00 P.M. I went back to the Commissary so that Clason could go to supper. We had a party tonight with two loaves of bread, jam, bologna and wine. After this we sang and had a good time.

["Right hand corner with milk" was written in code. I don't have a clue what he meant.]

2-4-1918 At 7:45 I reported to the Commissary at 7:45 and worked all morning giving out rations to the cook shacks. The day is a peach. I issued us our rations for the trip. It was a very nice afternoon with the sun shining at its best. I left the Commissary at 4:45. We had a very good supper of hamburg, mashed spuds, bread and cocoa. I will pack my barrack bag tonight and get an OK for the trip. We will carry with us two blankets, toilet articles, two days rations, an extra pair of shoes, underwear and three stockings. I had my hair cut baldy tonight. We had a feed tonight, the same as last night.

2-5-1918 I reported to the Commissary at 7:45 A.M. and worked sending out supplies to the shacks. We then started to store our baggage in the place. In the afternoon we worked hard finishing the storing post. I received a letter from Norma #22. It was a very good letter. The day is a peach, like a summer's day. About 4:45 I was relieved at the Commissary until 7:30 tomorrow. We had a very good supper of onions, potatoes, bread, bread pudding and coffee, considering we are moving tomorrow for the real trenches. We had another time like last night!

2-6-1918 At 7:30 I reported to the Commissary and helped in packing barrack bags in the Commissary. I worked hard and was relieved at the Commissary at 9:30 this morning. I reported back to the company and was detailed right away to clean up around the barracks. We are all packed and ready to leave here. It is a very nice day today. We have only sandwiches for dinner and the same for supper. At 1 P.M. we left Sartes for Liffol-le-Grande. We got there at 4:10 P.M. We hiked all the way and were very tired when we arrived. Then we got into train cars with 40 men in this car, some jam! We left here at 6:40 P.M. Before we left, I was looking over the town. We didn't sleep very much. It rained tonight. We had four rests from Sartes to Liffol-le-Grande.

[Liffol-le-Grande is in the Neufchateau township in the Lorraine region]

2-7-1918 The morning ration was cornwilly hash and four ounces of hard bread. I feel like I just came out of a football game, sore all over. One town we passed through was Mareuil-sur-Ourcq, then branched off towards Antilly, Voissy-Levingrer, Armoy-villers and landed at Soissons about 4:20 P.M. This place is all ruins and banged to pieces! It looks like every building has been hit by bombs or gun fire. We are not far from the front lines now. The place is a transportation point to the sector we cover. The place we are in is only about one and one-half kilos to Soissons, named Cuffies.

[Cuffies is in the Aisne department in Hauts-de-France].

The photo below of bombed out buildings was taken by Charles W. Robertson and provided by Ellen (Asplund) Racine of the Northborough Historical Society.

2-8-1918 It is a gray dull day, but warm. I went to the hospital for leg treatment. I came back and applied the medication given me. I went out for a walk all around through the dugouts and trenches. It was very interesting. We were in caves so dark and deep we had to light candles to see where we were going. I was with Joe Hobson all afternoon. After supper, the boys sneaked down to Soissons to look the town over. I had a big head tonight. We came back and got a lecture from Bates about tonight. I felt pretty bad about it.

2-9-1918 Reveille was at 6:00 A.M. It was a beautiful morning. I had another walk this morning in a different direction. Everything was ruined. We went through some of the German dugouts and underground passages. The battalion moved from here nearer to the front lines. We are in Tierny now. We saw the 103rd field artillery pass by us. While on my trip this morning, I saw bones, etc. There were plenty of graves! This afternoon we had some hike! We had only two rests all the way. We got to our destination about 5:30 P.M. Now this ends my experience today and no doubt I will sleep like a log. It is a very cloudy night.

[Knowing my grandfather, I think he was terribly distressed by this sight.]

2-10-1918 Reveille was at 6:30. It was a dull gray day. This place is batted to pieces also! I was on detail very nearly all morning. We had a fairly good dinner of beef stew, hard bread and coffee, considering what we are up against. I took a walk this afternoon around the vicinity, looking over the ruins, dugouts, etc. We had the pleasure of having supper with some French soldiers. I thought it was a very good supper. I came back about dusk. My squad was on guard for gas from 7 to 9 P.M. and 1 to 3 A.M. with three reliefs. It was a beautiful and rather a still night. Norma wrote to me on this day.

2-11-1918 Reveille was at 6:15. At 9:00 we fell in for a drill. We had a very interesting problem. There was an inspection of rifles and a gas tryout. At 2:00 in the afternoon we fell in and each squad was sent out in different directions on patrol and to map drawings. There was heavy bombardment today on the Front. We came back and were dismissed around 5:00. We went for a walk to the next village after supper. It was the first time I saw moving pictures in a long while. From where we were, we could see the bursting of shells. We came back about 9:00 and went to bed. It was very foggy tonight.

2-12-1918 Lincoln's birthday. Reveille was at 6:15 A.M. We fell in for drill at 9:00. Platoon leaders, lieutenants, etc. went to the Front Line trenches for instructions. We went on a hike, saw battery bases, dugouts, cemeteries and barbed wire entanglements. I also saw two German cemeteries. They had some beautiful floral pieces on top of the graves, made of beads of various colors. We came back and finished up on a few tryouts for gas. Recall was at 11:30. It was very foggy all morning. The sun is shining this afternoon. While out to drill this afternoon, we saw an air battle over head. The Hun airplane flew at high speed and got our observation balloon and the thing went up in flames. The balloon observer parachuted safely to the ground.

[Hun is a name for a German soldier.]

[Observation balloons were made of fabric and filled with hydrogen gas, which is why they would explode or go up in flames. Usually they were attached by a steel cable to a winch so they could be pulled back to the ground. Soldiers in the balloons could observe targets better and spot artillery. The soldiers had parachutes to escape if the balloon came under attack.][8]

The photo below of the ruins and cemetery was taken by Charles W. Robertson, provided courtesy of Ellen (Asplund) Racine, curator of the Northborough Historical Society.

2-13-1918 Reveille was at 4:30 A.M. We fell in and marched for a while. We put up three hundred meters of entanglement. It didn't take very long, but we plugged to get it done: four-point Hog, Iroquois wire and number eight wire. We were then told by the French to make a break as the Huns were sending up their balloons. We finished about 1:00 and marched back to our holes.

It was rainy and misty today. I signed over an allotment from Norma to father. Our lights were put out at 8:45 P.M. for we have to get up early tomorrow morning. There was heavy bombardment tonight. It rained very hard tonight.

[I think Walter meant that the Germans were sending up observation balloons so they could see the position of the American soldiers on the ground putting up the wire. I think that was the reason for the heavy bombardment that night.]

2-14-1918 St. Valentine's Day. Reveille was at 4:00 A.M. We fell in and marched to the place we were in yesterday morning and put up another three hundred meters of entanglement. The weather was very cloudy and raw. When we finished the job, we fell in and marched back to our holes at about 1:30. I could have eaten more for dinner which was beef stew, bread and coffee. Therefore, I dug into my reserve rations. We had inspections of our feet and coocoos. I have gotten frozen feet from our last heavy frost. I sent a couple of cards to Norma, Erhard and father. It was a beautiful evening with the stars shining brightly, but one of my blue nights. We will have to go to bed early as we are getting up early in the morning.

[*Coocoos* was a slang word for a small parasitic insect up to one-half inch or so in size.]

2-15-1918 Reveille was at 4:00 A.M. I was on kitchen detail all day from 4:00 A.M. to 9:00 P.M. There was a regular Fourth of July here at about 7:00 last night with an aerial fight over head. The anti-aircraft guns were pounding away at it. It was a beautiful day all day long with the sun shining. There were strong search lights last night tracing the airplanes. We went to bed early.

2-16-1918 Reveille was at 4:00 A.M. We fell in at 5:30 and marched to do more barbed wire entanglement. After we finished, we marched back to our holes. This morning there was aerial fighting again with shrapnel falling around. It was a very good clear day. I will rest all I can this afternoon, as I feel very tired. After supper, I went to the French canteen and bought some cocoa for twenty centimes. I will retire early tonight. It's rather cold and raw.

2-17-1918 Sunday Reveille was at 7:00 A.M. I sent a card to Norma and another to father. There was an aviation battle overhead. I saw an enemy airplane drop after a serious fight. We fell in with our rifles and gas masks and went to look over the airplane. There are plenty of troops at the Front. We passed the afternoon looking up at the airplanes overhead. It was a nice day today. We played a handful of whist this evening. There was heavy bombarding tonight with shells dropping everywhere. I will retire early. Norma writes today.

2-18-1918 Reveille was at 6:15 A.M. Drill was at 9:00 A.M. I worked on my sketches. We had another drill at 1:20, the same as this morning. I lost my gloves this afternoon. I was on detail loading wagons for the tear gas. We had another bad air battle this afternoon with about twelve Boche planes. I slept with only my overcoat. I could not get very comfortable. I'm getting a bad cold. It was a very pleasant day.

2-19-1918 Reveille was at 1:00 A.M. We had a "wonderful" breakfast of one piece of bread and a lukewarm cup of coffee. We will leave here at 3:30 A.M. for the Front Lines. It is a very clear morning. We got there about 5:00 A.M. It was some hike! There's heavy firing here by the artillery. I was detailed to go after the dinner of beef stew, bread and coffee for the troops. It was some hike again! Supper was tomato stew with crackers and coffee. I don't expect much sleep for five days. At just about 6:00 P.M. we got gassed. About 7:30 P.M. I went in to snooze, when all of a sudden we got orders to move out, as we were in a dangerous position for the German barrage. We hiked way back to a cave. I was very nearly all in from all the hikes today, but had enough guts to stick it out. I believe a prayer from across the sea helped me through. I'll repeat this again – a man can endure just about anything if he has hope of things getting better and has faith in God. I slept like a log. Norma writes today.

[Before reading this diary, I knew my grandfather was religious, but had no idea of his very deep faith. It has brought me closer to him although I won't see him again until the next life.]

2-20-1918 Stand to was from 5 to 7 A.M. We ate with D Company and had a very good bean stew with bread and coffee. I got an hour's sleep and was sent back to the Front later. It was a very good day. I am on the barbed wire detail for two hours this morning and again at 2:00 tonight. I feel pretty tired today. I was on the job at five to seven. I had to go quite a distance for a canteen of water. The moon was shining brightly tonight. I said a prayer to my Norma and then went to my bunk, ready to be called any minute. This ends my day's work so far. I left my initials in this cave where I slept on Antioch Farm. I read the "Mohnton Spirits on No Man's Land' today.

[There are limestone caves throughout this region where troops can take shelter when returning from the Front Line trenches. Some were a hundred feet down with stairs. See note after 3-7-1918.]

[Mohnton Spirits are Angel Spirits: Music of World War I. Supposedly the spirits come at midnight and by dawn they're gone again. Bob Seger wrote "No Man's Land" lyrics and Eric Bogle wrote lyrics "No Man's Land" commonly called "The Green Fields of France" about a dead soldier named Willie McBride].[9]

2-21-1918 Stand to was at 5 to 7. During this time, we put up entanglement wire. There were so many miscellaneous things that I did today. I hiked, stood guard, was detailed to get mess for dinner etc. We marched back to the Antioch Farm. We messed there for supper of beef stew which was the best we ate yet. This was with the D Company Platoon. From 6 to 9 P.M. we went out to dig trenches. It was a very quiet night, the first since we have come to this place. I felt pretty tired and slept quite comfortably. The weather today was a peach and we had a beautiful moonlight night.

[Walter was an artist and drew pictures, which he sent to his father, who designed wallpaper for a living.]

2-22-1918 Washington's Birthday. Stand to was from 5 to 6:15 A.M. This cave is very large – it's all limestone. We are wearing our gas masks and are at the alert all the time. We are only about one kilometer from the lines. There is not much firing today. It's very cloudy today. After supper, we passed through the trenches and put up wire entanglements from 6 to 9 P.M. Upon return, we went to roost. Tonight we were looking for coocoos and found only one of them. I slept pretty well.

2-23-1918 Stand to was from 5 to 6:15 A.M. After making my bunk, I policed around it and then read the "Worcester Gazette" dated January 22nd. This was about the first time I had a chance to see one. Both dinner and supper were very good today: steak, spuds and bread at noon and beef stew for supper. After mess, I laid down and rested. Following dinner, Sundin, Eugene (Walter's brother), and myself took a walk over to E Battery to visit. We met Jerry Laporte. We all enjoyed the trip. Today was hazy. We returned about 3:45. There wasn't much noise today. Once in a while there would be some noise. I retired at 9:30 P.M.

2-24-1918 Stand to was from 5 to 6:15 A.M. After mess, I had an opportunity to rest. There was heavy firing this morning on both sides, enough so it shook the cave we were in. Many landed close to us, the nearest one to me was about fifty-five yards away. This morning we went out and put up more barbed wire. In the afternoon we finished up laying one hundred meters of entanglement. Shells were landing all around us. The batteries were busy sending them back. We were detailed for guard duty tonight and were busy all the time. It seemed there was no let up of shelling. I received a letter from Norma tonight dated January 28th and one from Norton Company. I got a couple of cigars, blackstones, a treat to be sure. Now I will retire until called upon.

2-25-1918 Stand to was from 5 to 6:15 A.M. During stand to, we policed the cave that we were in. I was detailed to serve the mess for the platoon today. After that, I was detailed to fill the lister bag. During the afternoon, I was detailed to go for tar paper some distance from here. In the morning it was rather cloudy and dusty. In the afternoon it rained which made a disagreeable walk that was rather muddy, like sticky glue. We lost one of our lieutenants today. Evening mess was different for a change – turkey, mashed spuds, cranberries, bread and coffee. Some supper! The platoon was out on barbed wire entanglements this evening from 6 to 9 P.M. In the meantime I received a Valentine and "Norton Spirits" from my Norma. Sergeant Possen paid me a visit today. I will now retire, although I wish I could write a letter to Norma, but can not under the conditions we are in.

[Lister bags are canvas containers used especially for supplying troops in the field with chemically purified drinking water. The canvas weeps and provides some degree of evaporative cooling.]

2-26-1918 Stand to was from 5 to 6:15 A.M. In the meantime I was put on guard duty over the drinking tank to see that the boys didn't take any water out of the tank rather than the spout [which would cause dysentery]. I was relieved when stand to was over. Morning's mess was tomato soup with rice, bread and coffee. The day is a peach, very clear with a little frost during the night. I was on detail with pick and shovel, digging machine gun emplacements and digging another trench alongside the barbed wire entanglements to protect from the wire being cut. Noon mess was beef stew, bread and coffee. In the afternoon we did the same work as this morning. Boche balloons were up this afternoon for observation to locate our positions and to relay our positions to their artillery on the ground. Supper was beans, a pickle, bread and coffee. I received two letters from Norma dated February 3 and 5 a boiling out in the first but the second much better. I also got a card from Ma dated January 21. This afternoon shells landed not far from us. There was anti-aircraft shooting at the planes in the air. I finished letter #17 which is on its way to Norma.

[*Boche* is another name for German soldiers.]

[World War I balloons were oblong and more maneuverable and hardy than hot air balloons. They were made of tightly woven fabric that could take plenty of hits without splitting. However, the gas available in WWI was hydrogen gas, which would explode in a fireball, so fighter planes usually avoided them.][10]

2-27-1918 Stand to was at 5 to 6:15. During this time, we policed the cave. I was on the pick and shovel detail this morning, digging a trench and machine gun emplacements. In the afternoon we went out to complete our day's labor. The weather wasn't very promising this morning but turned out to be excellent. There were only a few shells today – otherwise it was very quiet. I felt like working today, because it was soft digging. For supper we had tomato soup, which was well camouflaged all right, with bread and coffee. I felt good when I got two more letters #23 and #24 from Norma. I sent the #17 letter I wrote last night to Norma. The mail service was cut off until we get to our next destination.

2-28-1918 Stand to was from 5 to 6:15 during which time we policed the cave. I am detailed to serve this morning's mess. It's raining out and very muddy. In the morning I was on trench detail. We are leaving here, getting prepared this afternoon. Afternoon mess was very good – steak, gravy, spuds, bread and coffee. We cleaned up the cave. The French sent over a heavy barrage of fire this evening. It was some sight – believe me! At 10:15 we left Antioch Farm and arrived here in Tierny-Sourny at 11:15 P.M. I was put on Klaxan hour.

[Klaxan was the trademark for an electrically operated horn or warning signal.]

[Tierny-Sourny is in the department of Aisne in the region of Picardie in the district of Soissons, which is in the north of France 62 miles northeast of Paris. This is the Hauts-de-France.]

3-1-1918 We got up at 9:00 A.M. It was a very nice day this morning, but this afternoon it is snowing, the first we have had for a very long time. We laid around all afternoon and rolled our packs. Dinner was at 3:30 P.M. roast beef, spuds, tomato, bread and coffee. We went to the moving pictures this afternoon, such as they were. There was no supper, but from 7:45 to 10:00 P.M. we had a stiff hike to another large cave about 40 feet deep with all electric lights. I am bunking at the extreme end of the cave. Lights went out at 10:40 P.M. Everybody is scratchy tonight. I slept very well through the night, although it is very close in here. The name of this place is Lafaux.

[The soldiers were most likely scratchy from lice or coocoos in the trenches or the caves.]

[Lafaux is in the French region Picardie, part of the district of Soissons in the Hauts-de-France region.]

[Some movies of the period were Charlie Chaplin, *J'Accuse* about men who met in the trenches, a documentary titled *Kitchener's Great Army in the Battle of the Somme*, *Fields of Honor*, *Go West, Young Man*, *Lonesome Luke*, *The Birth of a Nation* about the Civil War and Klu Klux Klan, *Intolerance: Love's Struggle Throughout the Ages*, *The Poor Little Rich Girl*, *The Mystery of the Leaping Fish*, and *Frankenstein*, a Fatty Arbuckle comedy named *Moonshine* to name a few.][11]

3-2-1918 We got up about 7:30 A.M. and were put on detail to help get our rolling kitchen placed so we could get something to eat. There was no breakfast this morning but at 1:30 P.M. we were served beans, bread and coffee. There was a light coating of snow on the ground this morning and it was a rather cold snappy day outside. I left my initials in the cave over where I slept. I sent no. 17 letter to Norma, 10 pages in all that I wrote on February 27. This is about the only day we really didn't do any work. I shaved tonight. You would laugh yourself sick to see the boys looking for the pesky coocoos. There is not much more for today's diary, so I will go to bed.

3-3-1918 Sunday. I got up about 7:30. There wasn't anything to do today, except to lay around. It was a dismal day, muddy and sloppy out. It's very close in this cave and I didn't sleep very well last night. There seemed to be something wrong about the mess most all of the time – no seasoning – beef stew, bread and coffee. This afternoon I cleaned up my rifle. I subscribed for a paper called "Stars and Stripes" which cost four francs for three months. I will send it to Norma once a week. Supper was beef stew, bread and coffee – much better than dinner. We are enjoying ourselves fairly well, playing cards and telling stories, etc. Chasing rats is a specialty. I stripped tonight – the first time since we left Sartes. I oiled my feet and went hunting for coocoos. I said a prayer for home.

3-4-1918 Reveille was at 4:30 A.M. Mess was at 5:00 and we are getting very small rations these days – bacon, bread and coffee. The boys went out on barbed wire detail this morning. I stayed in and helped sweep up our section of the cave. After finishing, I slept a little. It was rainy out all day. Noon mess was roast beef, one spoonful of mashed spuds, bread and coffee - just enough to get a taste. The boys are not satisfied with the quantity of food given us lately. During the afternoon, we had an inspection of our rifles. For supper we had hash, bread and coffee, worse than at noon. Talk about lousy – whew!! I'm hungry enough to eat anything. The boys dug out for the French kitchens when they finished eating in order to get what they had left over. After supper, we played a game of hearts and I won out. It's now 7:30 PM almost time to go to sleep. I wanted to write to Norma, but didn't have any paper. I wrote #18 letter to Norma after hunting up some paper.

3-5-1918 Reveille was at 4:45 A.M. I was detailed this morning on a wiring party, putting up barbed wire entanglements for about one hundred twenty meters. It was a dismal cold and wet morning, very disagreeable moving to do any work. The roads were sloppy and muddy. We came back about 10:30 to the cave, quite a hike to the destination, say about three miles. While on my trip, I saw apple trees deliberately cut down by the Germans when they occupied the area. There is plenty of hill climbing here. The afternoon turned out to be very nice and sunny. We played cards for a short while this afternoon and then rested until supper. I was issued a cap tonight.

3-6-1918 Reveille was at 6:45. The bacon was in a very bad mess, leaving the platoon in a grumble towards the cook shack. I was on detail serving the mess for today. It was a very nice warm day with the sun shining all morning. For dinner we had a fairly good beef stew, bread and coffee. At 12:30 P.M. we prepared ourselves for a hike to Maraville for a shower bath. [It is in northeast France in the department of Meuse in the region of Lorraine 235 kilometers from Paris.] It was worth the trip for the bath, now a very complicated shower-bath house consisting of twenty shower heads with dressing rooms. It was a portable French Red Cross bath heated by a huge boiler on wheels. We were given French underwear and stockings. We were glad to get rid of our old ones as they were very crummy. Three platoons will leave here tonight but the 4th F Company Platoon will remain until further notice. There is not much more news for today.

3-7-1918 Reveille was at 7:00 A.M. I didn't get up until the mess came. The cook shack is about one and one-half kilos from here. I took it easy all morning until about 11:00. Then I cleaned my rifle and shaved. I spent the afternoon walking around and looking over the dugouts, etc. It was a very nice warm day. We watched the battery fire a few shells over the lines. It was some noise! We had "supposed steak", a spoonful of mashed spuds, no bread and coffee. After eating what little I got, I went over to the French kitchen and got all the beans I could get. They are certainly good cooks! I met an English speaking French man and he told me many experiences he went through, the last one was being gased with mustard gas. We moved to another cave that held nearly 3400 men.

[From my undergraduate major of geography and geology, I know that there are a lot of beautiful limestone caves in the Champagne (northeast) area of France. Many of these were reduced to ruins during World War I. Walter even mentioned in one entry that he left his initials in one of the caves. Wikipedia states that ancient crypts carved in the fourth century underneath the beautiful high Gothic Cathedral Notre-Dame de Reims were rediscovered in the tenth century. Many French kings were crowned in this cathedral. Various fires during the ages led to renovations to the cathedral. During World War I, the Champagne region in northeast France was heavily bombarded and in ruins. Numerous vineyards were destroyed. The passageways and cellars beneath the cathedral housed millions of bottles of champagne from the champagne houses in the region. The caves beneath the cathedral and in the region were used to shelter thousands of people from civilians to soldiers during the war. For a time it was used as a hospital. Reims is in the heart of Champagne and was an important landmark on the Western Front. So these caves that existed for centuries housed the Allied troops during the war.][12]

3-8-1918 There was no reveille this morning, but we got up when mess came. We had bacon, prunes, bread and coffee – a fairly good feed. I was detailed for the mess today. It was a very nice day. There was plenty of anti-aircraft shooting at the airplanes. I saw a wonderful exhibition of two airplanes fighting in the air. I spent the afternoon sight seeing around the different caves, one cave only a short distance from here. We were not allowed to enter in there, because there are so many dead bodies buried there. After supper, I went over to see Emile Lauste of the 118th E regiment infantry. I was with him all evening and we had a very pleasant time telling stories, etc. It was about 11:00 P.M. before I went to bed. I slept fairly well last night.

3-9-1918 There was no reveille this morning, but when the mess came we got up. After breakfast, I came out from the "Underworld" to get some fresh air. It's not a pleasant smell in these caves. We had a fair dinner of beef stew, bread and coffee. I spent the afternoon outside taking in some fresh air. I saw a few air battles, but none seemed to be effective, but were still very interesting. We had something different for supper – salmon mashed in spuds with bread and coffee. I had a very nice time amongst some noncoms French with singing, laughter and funny stories. It was a very sociable way to pass the time away. A big night! It was 1:00 before I hit the hay.

[Noncoms refers to noncommisioned officers.]

3-10-1918 We had reveille when we got our mess. It was supposed to be lamb stew, but I failed to see the lamb – it must have been camouflaged. It is a very nice day with the sun shining. I took a walk by myself partly for my own personal benefit, but also because I felt very blue today. For noon mess we had hamburg hash with bread and coffee which was fair but not what it could have been. I spent the afternoon outside the cave and then decided to take a bath while I had the chance. I was with Lauste all afternoon. After supper, the French sergeants set me up on another feed of beans, bread and coffee. I had a swell time, the same as last night. There was a barrage by the French tonight. I wrote #19 letter to Norma tonight four pages long. Norma received this letter on April 14, 1918.

[As his granddaughter, I feel that he often suffered from depression because of what he experienced in the war.]

3-11-1918 There was no reveille this morning, but we got up when the breakfast came. Afterwards, I went for a bath where I got new underwear, stockings and another cap. I will use this one for a night cap. There's nothing like a nice bath! It's like a summer day, nice and warm. The 118th regiment of the French pulled out this morning for a rest period further back from the Front Lines. I was detailed to take the dixies over to the cook shack about two kilos from here. While walking over there, I witnessed a few aerial battles overhead. At present I am sitting directly on top of a large railroad tunnel which the Germans destroyed. The French are rebuilding it over again and are about two and one-half kilos through it. Supper was beef stew which didn't suit me, so I went to the French kitchen and got a good feed. I made an acquaintance with a French sergeant who could speak fairly good English. I passed a very pleasant evening with him. This sergeant is in the 264th regiment 13th company. I didn't sleep well tonight, as it was very close in the cave.

[*Dixie* was a trench slang for the tin soldiers (or food containers) used in cooking. *Doolally* is a trench slang for an insane person.]

3-12-1918 I was put on guard from 2 to 3 A.M. I got up in time for mess. I was very happy to get two packages containing fudge, square candy and chewing gum in one parcel and cookies, five bars of chocolate, sardines, salt, cough candy, one towel and some more fudge from my girl Norma, as well as two letters #29 and # 30 from her. The funny part was to get it all in the same bunch. To top it off I received one letter from Maurice, one from Lucius and one from Westfield. I was a very happy boy, but very lonesome. During the afternoon, I was detailed to lug the dixies back to the kitchen. It is a very nice pleasant day and warm. We had beans, bread and coffee tonight, a little better in the feeds. I was issued iron rations after supper. I called on the French sergeant and passed away another pleasant evening. I got a postal from Ed, which I couldn't make out until later, when I found out it was from Ed Martin.

3-13-1918 There was no reveille, but we got up when mess arrived: bacon, bread and coffee again – just about every morning since January. I went back to sleep again until noon mess. It was a fair dinner of loose hamburg, mashed spuds, bread and coffee. The day was fine and breezy. At the present time, I am sitting on an apple tree stump which the Germans deliberately destroyed by cutting it down. Not one tree is left standing on the site. There are shell holes too numerous to mention in this area. There is a church to my left battered to ruins. The graveyard is turned upside down. For supper we had stew, a mystery, but very tasty, with bread and coffee. I am having a hard time trying to get writing paper. Finally, I found some so I could write #20 letter to Norma, answering her last three in this one. I received #28 letter from Norma.

3-14-1918 There was no reveille, but we got up when the mess arrived. We policed our sector of the cave. I am slightly infected with gas, mostly from the cave. We had a formation this morning at 9:30 A.M.– something to take up our time so we won't be idle. I was detailed to go after the mess for dinner. I have had the runs pretty much lately. This morning it was very foggy, but the sun came out in the afternoon and it was warm. I wrote to Lucius and Mrs. Reagan this afternoon. We got orders to roll our packs and moved from this cave at 6:30 P.M. We arrived at a much larger cave about two kilos from here where there are electric lights. There are some beautiful sculptures in the wall of this cave. Lights went out at 10:00 P.M.

[Again, Walter is an artist and would naturally notice such beautiful sculptures on the walls.]

[Canaries were used in cages often by miners digging the trenches to test the air after explosions. They must have, or should have, had them in the caves also.]

3-15-1918 Stand to was from 4:45 to 6:30 A.M. After mess at 7:00 P.M., we went on a working party digging and cleaning up a line of trenches. We ate our dinner in the trenches. We saw a Boche plane get hit and come down with a crash. It was a very nice day, rather breezy. We put in eight hours of work today digging and picking. We saw a skeleton or rather a skull from a human body. We came back about 4:00. It was very dark coming into the cave. The lights came on about 5:15. We were on guard tonight from 9:00 P.M. to 9:00

P.M. tomorrow night. I am on the first relief 9:00 to 11:00 P.M. and then again from 3:00 to 6:20 A.M.

[The Boche plane was a German plane.]

3-16-1918 I am on guard from 3:00 to 6:20 A.M. and not feeling well today. The air in the cave is very bad and it's very damp in here. It is a very pleasant day outside. Morning breakfast was very skimpy bacon, bread and coffee. I slept until dinner which was also skimpy – one spoonful of hamburg, a spoonful of spuds, one piece of bread and a cup of coffee. At about 1:30 P.M. I went out, cleaned up and shaved. I am pretty sick – it must be the grippe. I was put on guard at the Colonel's Headquarters for one hour from 6:00 to 7:00 P.M. There was heavy firing at times, but otherwise quiet. This was one of the worst nights I've spent here in France, thinking of home and Norma.

3-17-1918 Sunday. St. Patrick's Day. Stand to was from 4:45 to 6:30. I went back and laid down again to sleep until the church services woke me up. The chapel is only about thirty feet from my bunk. I heard both of the calls for services from where I slept. I am feeling somewhat better today, but still have a bad headache and my lungs feel sore when I cough. The Germans sent over gas last night and a barrage. I had trouble again over the noon mess of salmon mixed with spuds, bread and coffee. I took in some fresh air this afternoon, then came back and laid down again. Supper was salmon, turnips, bread and coffee. There are no writing materials anywhere. I wanted to write a letter in the worst way to my girl over there. Writing letters has been stopped, no more censoring, until later.

[A barrage is sustained artillery fire at a series of points along a line.]

[All letters were censored by junior officers before being sent to make sure that the soldiers didn't say something that would give away military secrets, locations, and casualties. Soldiers knew this, so they were careful not to say such sensitive things or their letters would not be sent. They were stamped if the letters were safe to send. They were censored again when they reached Britain before being sent to the United States.]

3-18-1918 Stand to was from 4:45 to 6:30 A.M. During this time, we policed around our bunks. After stand to, I was detailed to get the mess. For breakfast we had a greasy lamb stew. My stomach was too proud to recognize it. I ate just the bread and coffee. Then I laid down for a little while. Because it is quite unsafe to do any fatigue work outside in the open, they keep us in the cave as much as possible. I went outside to get some fresh air. It is a beautiful day today. I took my rifle out and cleaned it thoroughly. It sure was a mess, as the cave is very damp. Dinner was very satisfying: roast beef, mashed potatoes, a big piece of punk. After dinner, I took my blankets outside to air them out. I laid around in the sun all afternoon. I enjoyed the can of sardines Norma sent me, along with the supper of stewed tomatoes, bread and coffee. I shared the sardines with C.H.C. They relieved us of one of our blankets. I slept fine.

3-19-1918 Norma's Birthday. I said a prayer for my girl Norma for her birthday. Stand to was from 4:45 to 6:30 A.M. We policed around our bunks. It is rainy today and getting muddy. After cleaning up and shaving, I rested a little and was then detailed to get the mess for dinner. After dinner of salmon mashed with spuds plus bread and coffee, we were given plenty of details. We are leaving here tonight. Things are very quiet on the front lines today. We turned in our ammunition and extra shoes. We were issued new rations to carry on our hike. We worked around the cave, cleaning up until it was time to leave at 9:15 P.M. On our journey, we passed through Neuville, Margival until we came to Cuffies. It was a pretty wet night and sloppy walking.

[Neuville is in Hauts-de-France, Margival is in the department of Aisne in the district of Soissons, and Cufffies is in the department of Aisne located in the township of Soissons-Nord (north) in Hauts-de-France.]

3-20-1918 We arrived in Cuffies at 3:30 A.M. and went back to the same barracks that we left on February 9, 1918. I slept until 11:00 A.M. We were told to roll our packs and then ate our breakfast at 2:00 P.M. I was put on guard duty over the Company's property. The Company went ahead of us and we were left behind to guard the property. I got a new pair of spiral leggings today. It is a dull dismal day and very muddy. We met the rest of the outfit at 1:30 A.M. and then hiked to Mercin-et-Vaux. It was about 3:30 A.M. when we arrived there. We were entrained at this place, given a cup of supposed coffee and one apple from the Y.M.C.A. I am packed into a box car with forty-four men, a pretty tight squeeze! It is a nice moonlight night.

[Mercin-et-Vaux is in the Aisne department in the township of Soissons-Sud (south) in the district of Soissons.]

3-21-1918 We laid over in Brienne le Chateau. We were given a cup of coffee here and corned beef hash with plenty of punk for breakfast. It is a great day – warm with the sun shining. I rode on the flat cars and enjoyed the scenery. We passed through Champagne which is named for its champagne vineyards. It is some place! CHC and myself slept on the flat cars until 5:00 A.M. We got a boiling out for not being near the Company when they pulled out. All movements are made by moonlight or early in the morning.

3-22-1918 We landed here in Bar-sur-Aube, a beautiful town which is very neat throughout. We were given a flop in the attic of one of these houses and slept until 11:30 A.M. For breakfast we had cornwilly [made from corned beef], three pieces of bread and coffee. We took a walk around the town – it was a treat to get into the city. The day was a peach with the sun shining brightly.

In the photo below Walter is the soldier on the left and I think the other soldier is Charlie. [Bar-sur-Aube is located in the department of Champagne-Ardenne region in the Grande-Est northeast area of France, 187 kilometers from Paris.]

3-23-1918 Reveille was at 6:30 A.M. For breakfast we had tomato stew, bread and coffee. We policed around the bunks, washed up and cleaned our rifles. We saw the batteries pass by: A, B, C, and D Headquarters, etc. Formation was at 10:00 A.M. for short finger inspection, feet inspection, as well as inspection of rifles and other equipment. For noon mess we had a soup, tomatoes, bread and coffee. In the afternoon CHC and myself walked around town and tried to enjoy ourselves, but it's hell to be broke and lonesome! The weather was a peach. We had a lousy supper – one jam sandwich, one piece of bread and cup of coffee. After supper, we went for a walk again and felt the same as this afternoon. The band played a few pieces for us. It certainly felt good to hear some music. I will retire early. God be with my Norma.

3-24-1918 Palm Sunday. I got up at 9:30 A.M. It was another beautiful day. We cleaned and policed the place. Then C.H.C. and myself took a walk. We got orders to roll our packs to move at 1:30 P.M. from here in Bar-sur-Aube. It was very good hiking. We won't get any eats until we hit the next stopping place. This place we hit is Lignol, a very neat little village. At 6:00 P.M. we had cornwilly hash, hard bread and coffee. We are billeted in a barn. When we arrived here, C.H.C. and myself took a sponge bath and felt fine afterwards. Then we took a stroll in the moonlight and turned in at 9:30 P.M. I slept very nicely. J.H. is feeling good.

3-25-1918 One year ago today Eugene, myself and the rest of our Company were called out for service. I came back from New Hampshire on March 25, 1917. This morning I went on bridge guard. Reveille was at 5:00 A.M. After mess at 5:30 A.M., we were ordered to roll our packs by 7:30 to move onward. We passed through Lavilleneuve, a very quiet little farm village with good farming throughout this place. It was a beautiful day. We stopped in Jurennecourt, another pretty place and billeted in a barn. C.P.C. and myself went to take a swim in a running stream. It was the Doubs River. After dinner, I went out for a stroll and laid down under a pine tree and fell asleep. Afterwards, I went for a haircut. We had cornwilly stew, one-half box of bread and no coffee for supper, I stayed around my bunk ready to go to bed.

[Lavilleneuve is located in the Hauts-de-France in the north east of France.]

3-26-1918 Reveille was at 4:45 A.M. I was detailed to the soup guns at 5:30
A.M. We rolled our packs and were ready on the march at 7:10 A.M. We passed
through the towns of Sixfontaines, Meures, Morault, Cologne, and Bosseval-
et-Briancourt. We stopped and ate our hard bread between this town and Chantraines. It was a very good day for hiking – it was a corking hike. We arrived in
Chantraines at about 3:00 A.M. I made my bunk and laid down for a while. Everything was very dirty and dusty from the roads. For supper we had our fill of
roast beef hash, boiled onions, bread and coffee. I felt very sore and very tired.
I will retire early. I saw Red Robinson, the first time since Westfield.

[*Corking* is slang for extremely fine.]

[Bosseval-et-Briancourt is located in the department of Ardennes in the
Champagne-Ardenne region in northeast France.]

[Chantraines is a small village in the department of Haute-Marne in the
region Champagne-Ardenne in the Grand-Est region of northeast France.]

3-27-1918 Reveille was at 6:00. We prepared for our final hike from Chantraines to Blancheville, Andelot to Rimaucourt, only about eight kilometers.
We had a fair breakfast of bacon, rice, bread and coffee. I passed the morning
looking over the place and went to wash and shave, etc. At 2:00 we had a fair
dinner of beef stew, bread and coffee. I went for another walk and saw many
Chinese laborers and German prisoners. I went through a charcoal shop,
where the girls working there were very dirty, do believe me! This is a transportation point for the 26th Division. It was a pleasant day, but was very dusty
on the roads, worse than at the border. I received two boxes from Norma, one
with gloves, the other with toilet articles, cigars and tobacco – very needed
things at this time. I was very short on tobacco. I received letter #22 from
Norma, one from the Red Cross, and one from Norton's.

3-28-1918 Reveille was at 4:45 A.M. I was put on detail all morning loading
baggage at Manois. Things were in a pretty mess here, but it was a great day
to work. It was a pity the way they use the mail for the boys – I saw a good example of it at this place. I didn't eat any dinner but, I did drink some booze
and was stewed. What an awful afternoon I put in this life! I returned to camp
about time for supper. Joe Hobson brought my supper to me. I was put on
three details after supper: first, lugging blankets, then water for the kitchen,

and then cleaning up. I stayed in the barracks as I felt very blue tonight over numerous things. I'm in Rimaucourt at this time. I'm finished for the day.

[When he said he was stewed, I think Walter meant drunk.]

3-29-1918 Reveille was at 6:00 A.M. There was plenty of work today, leaving me a bit behind in my diary. It's rainy and sloppy out today. I bought a few necessities that I needed. I wrote #21 letter to Norma tonight and received #33 from her.

3-30-1918 I got up at 8:00 A.M. It is raining today. I cleaned up, shaved and then worked all day on details, preparing to move forward to the Front lines again. There's not much to tell about today, except a short talk by Colonel Sheldon. It was a disagreeable day to work. We are moving tomorrow. I played cards until 11:00 P.M. I retired quite late, because it was our last day before going to the Front.

3-31-1918. Easter Sunday. Reveille was at 4:00 A.M. and mess was at 4:30 A.M. We rolled our packs and were on the move to the Front lines again at 6:00 A.M. We had plenty of details. Trucks took us to the Front lines through Liffol le Grand and Neufchateau to Vignot. After that, we hiked which left us pretty tired after such a long hike and getting up so early. At 4:00 P.M. we had our iron rations. There was heavy firing while entering the reserve lines, which was our first stop. This was at 10:15 P.M. We ate a lunch of what we picked up when we got here. The rations came in very handy. Believe me, we were hungry! Some Easter Sunday! It was raining to beat the cars all day long. I feel very tired tonight. This place we are in is Fremereville-sous-les-Cotes which is about seven kilometers from the Front Lines

[Iron rations were emergency rations of preserved meat, cheese, a biscuit, tea, sugar and salt.]

[Fremereville-sous-les-Cotes is in the department of Meuse in the region of Lorraine in Grand Est in north eastern France about 242 kilometers, or 150 miles, east of Paris.]

4-1-1918 April Fool's Day. I slept until about 10:30 A.M. Our mess was our iron rations. We went over to the next town Gironville about one kilometer from here and got some eggs for seventy-two cents a dozen. They sure did taste good, the first I have had for a long time. It was raining today. We had a wild time today – the boys sure did get the benefits out of the wine shops in town! The captain put a stop to it, for things were too loud to suit him. We rolled our packs to move, but when nightfall came, we were told to unroll our packs and to go to sleep here. The rolling kitchen came in tonight quite late.

4-2-1918 I got up at 10:00 A.M. and had a sandwich for mess around 12:00 with tomato soup, bread and coffee. I cleaned up and shaved myself. It was raining this morning, but cleared up this afternoon. We played cards all afternoon. After supper mess of beef stew, bread and coffee, we played cards until 9:00 P.M. There was bombarding in the adjoining town tonight. It's strange that this town is untouched by shells, being so near the lines. We retired about 10:30 P.M.

4-3-1918 Stand to was at 6:00 A.M. We policed around the place. After making my bunk, we were ordered to roll our packs to move to Fort de Liouville which was built in 1876. It was some fort! It had very good quarters of iron bunks with mattresses, places to store our rifles, and a very good place to eat our meals. It's only one kilo from the Front Lines. We no more than got our bunks made and somewhat settled, when the order came to roll our packs and move back to our previous quarters. On our way back, we went through shell fire that was very close. It was a narrow escape with shells landing all around us. This was the closest they've come to me so far. It was the most exciting time since I've been in the lines. I was with my corporal at this time of shelling. We arrived safely in the town of Fremereville-sous-les-Cotes. From there, we passed through the towns of Gironadins and St. Julien to Liouville. We are resting here for the night.

[The Fort de Liouville was built to defend the department of Meuse, which was only one kilometer from the Front Lines.]

4-4-1918 Stand to was from 5:00 to 6:30 A.M. We policed our bunks during the stand to. We had a very good breakfast of Campbell's tomato soup, hard bread and coffee. We went back to sleep until noon. We had a fair dinner of loose hamburg, mashed spuds, hard bread and coffee. We played cards until 3:30 P.M. I wrote letter #22 to Norma. The weather was fair but it rained at times – an undecided day. I went on guard duty from 4:00 until 6:00 P.M. Supper was a very good prepared soup with hard bread and coffee. We were then ordered to roll our packs and prepare to leave at 8:00 P.M. to be nearer the Front Lines. We arrived there about 9:15 P.M. in barracks situated in a large barge in thick woods for shelter. I went on guard duty from 10:00 to 12:00 P.M.

4-5-1918 About 2:30 in the early part of the morning, there was some heavy firing. I went on guard duty again from 4:00 to 6:00 A.M. I slept until 10:00 A.M. and then went on guard again until 12:00. It was a beautiful day. Charlie Campbell and myself went after water which was about a twenty-five minute walk from our camp. We had to pass through an open field observed by the enemies' observation balloons. They fired a few shells over us while we were drawing the water. We got back in time for mess of beef and soup with bread and coffee. Charlie and I came out of the barracks and passed a few minutes in the woods. At 10:30 P.M, Charlie and I were pulled out of bed on the ration detail.

4-6-1918. Charlie and I returned from ration detail about 2:30 A.M. this morning. I had a light lunch with Charlie and then retired. Stand to was from 6:00 to 6:30 A.M. I was very tired and slept until 9:00 A.M. I had to rise for mess of rice with Jewish bread and coffee. Afterwards, we had inspection of gas masks. Charlie and myself went down to the washers to clean up and shave. We returned at 1:30 P.M. for mess at 2:30 of steak, spuds and Jewish hard bread with coffee. We spent the afternoon in the woods roaming and lounging around to pass the time. There was plenty of noise from the batteries from both sides, not far from our camp. Supper consisted of oxtail soup, Jewish bread and coffee. We rolled our packs and pulled out at 8:00 P.M. for Liouville Fort where we arrived at 11:15 P.M.. We had the same bunks we had before. It was some hike! I slept like a log.

4-7-1918 Seven years ago today I left home. Today is Sunday - we got up at 9:00 A.M. and had breakfast at 9:30 A.M. We were sent on ration detail to Gironville for the troops at Liouville Fort. I was pretty tired. It was raining pretty hard. We had a light lunch with the platoon there and returned to Liouville. We got back about 3:15 A.M. and there was bombarding from the Front as we were coming back in. We played cards pretty late to pass the time. I got to bed pretty late and slept pretty well. One year ago today the U.S. declared war on Germany, because of German submarine attacks on U.S. merchant ships. Norma wrote a letter dated April 7, 1918 that I received much later.

[Walter noted that he left home seven years ago. I don't know what he was doing until he volunteered for the Massachusetts National Guard to serve in 1916 in Texas and New Mexico fighting the Mexican rebels under Poncho Villa.]

4-8-1918 Reveille was at 6:30 A.M. We policed the place, falling in with rifles at 8:00 A.M. after breakfast. We had a school on automatic rifles in the Fort. In case of heavy bombardment, we were shown our positions some sixty feet below the ground well protected. It is raining today and very foggy. In the afternoon we had another drill and were given our positions for gun teams in case of an attack. I have a fair position near the observation post. This afternoon there was a raw wind blowing. I spent the evening reading the "Daily Mail" and then went to bed. I rested comfortably.

4-9-1918 Reveille was at 5:30. We policed around our bunks, etc. At 7:00 A.M. I was detailed to go after our Automatic ammunition – 4096 rounds. I went way down a hole to the magazine for it and passed by the electric lighting station. It was very interesting going through alley ways which were very nearly all concrete. It was raining and very foggy today. I wrote my #2 letter to Erhard Kjellberg. After this, I enjoyed a very good shower bath in the Fort about 2:45 P.M. It was built for six persons. I started to write a letter to Mrs. Aldrich but will have to finish it tonight. The Germans attacked us heavily with shells landing in the Fort now at 3:00 P.M. Later I finished the letter to Mrs. Aldrich, one to Frenchy, a card to Kate Manning and one to Grundstrom. I was on detail from 11:35 P.M. to 1:45 A.M. for rations. Some job!

4-10-1918 Reveille was at 6:00 A.M. I think breakfast mess was a rather small feed of syrup, bread and coffee. We fell in for drill in Automatic gun team combat formations. We took the rifle apart and put it back together again. I practiced with the team loading clips, etc. We were dismissed at 9:30 A.M. and were then put on another detail carrying wood from the foot of the hill. Because it was very cloudy, we were able to accomplish the job. A very heavy barrage from both sides was going on continuously for mostly two and one-half hours. The Huns tried an attack, but were checked in good style. Dinner of steak, bread and coffee was very good, but what a slim amount we got. After dinner, we went out on detail carrying wood again. It was very foggy and misty out. I laid down for a while. We had a very good supper of beef stew with rice, bread and unsweetened coffee. We went out to our positions about 8:30 P.M. tonight. Then we went to bed.

4-11-1918 Reveille was at 6:00 A.M. We had automatic rifle instructions – the first part was setting up the exercise. It was a peach of a day and warm. I received #31 letter from Norma dated February 24, 1918, one from Dad dated February 16, 1918 and one from Irving. I also received a good sized welcome box from Mrs. Reagan, containing two bars of soap, two towels, one tube of toothpaste, one shaving cream, two packages of tobacco, one cigar, two candles, a box of candy, one Peters chocolate, gum, clipping and pipe cleaners. I was in need of all of these items at this time. The boys played cards in the afternoon. Evening was at the game tonight. I was on gas sentry from 11:00 P.M. to 1:00 A.M. The wind was blowing hard tonight.

4-12-1918 I came off of guard duty at 1:00 A.M. this morning and fooled around until almost 3:00 A.M. when I jumped into bed. I got up at 5:30 A.M. We had a very skimpy breakfast of one piece of bread and coffee, but a fellow can't kick – it doesn't pay! On my way down to mess, the gas alert was sounded which kind of took us by surprise. I went back for my G.B.R. as I only had my French gas mask with me. Then the order to remove masks was sounded. During formation, we were given instructions on automatic rifles again for the benefit of new men on how to use this rifle in case we are barraged and not able to continue. It is a beautiful warm day today. Dinner was steak, spuds and coffee. We fell in to the same routine of duty in barbed wiring, portable fences, for three and one-half hours of work. In the afternoon we had automatic rifle schooling again. There was a heavy barrage on our left. Four platoons of H Company with Lieutenant Knight were killed with grenades. We took our positions to defend the Fort at 9:00 P.M. There was a beautiful sight of barrage with heavy fighting also.

[According to Wikipedia, on April 10, 12, and 13,, the 104th infantry regiment, of which Walter and Eugene were members, was bombarded and attacked by the Boche, as related by Walter in his diary. They were in Bois Brule, which was near Apremont in the Ardennes Forest in the Champagne-Ardenne region. Some of the advanced trenches were not held strongly by the Americans, so the Germans gained some ground. During the day, the troops were sent out to add more barbed wire fencing before the counterattack. The 104th infantry regiment counterattacked the Boche in hand-to-hand combat with bayonets. They were able to drive out the Germans without serious loss of life. However, as related by Walter above, four platoons of H Company were killed with grenades.][13]

4-13-1918 Reveille was at 6:00 A.M. At 8:00 A.M. we fell in for automatic rifle instructions until 9:00 A.M. Then we went out doing barbed wiring until 11:00 A.M. We played cards until dinner mess. We played cards until 1:30 P.M. and then went out to finish the barbed wiring we started in the morning. We played cards again until 3:00 P.M. We went for a bath which sure was fine. Supper of beef stew and coffee was at 5:30. After supper, I witnessed another heavy barrage in the same place as last night. It was a little hazier day so you couldn't see a great distance. I started #23 letter to Norma. I was on ration detail tonight and lugged the beef back here. Afterwards, I finished the letter to Norma. This is all for tonight so good night. A prayer goes with my letter.

4-14-1918 Sunday. Reveille was at 8:00 A.M. Although there was no formation this morning, we had inspection of our quarters by the French captain and Lieutenant Bird. I shaved, cleaned up and washed my O.D. Shirt, the first time since I got it. It certainly needed it. It was a very pleasant day but a little windy. It was very quiet on the lines this morning. After my washing was done, I slept a little. Dinner was a fairly good beef stew with bread and coffee. I rested for the afternoon until 5:00 P.M. This afternoon the Germans sent over some shells in answer to those we sent them yesterday. Supper was stew with bread in it and coffee. I used my coffee with supper to clean out my mess kit. We have a splendid view of the Front Lines from Liouville Fort where we are stationed. It was a very lonesome day for me especially today. A married woman asked the photographer here how much his pictures were. He said 2.50 a dozen. She said she would be back later as she didn't have enough. We've been living very comfortably in this Fort for one week. I wrote #3 letter to Dad.

4-15-1918 Reveille was at 6:00. For mess we had only one piece of bread and coffee. We policed around the quarters. At 8:00 A.M. we were detailed to clean out a trench that a shell hit previously. It was a rainy and disagreeable day. We returned from detail at 11: A.M. and rested until dinner. During the time we were cleaning out the trench, the Germans sent shells over but they were beyond us. Dinner was beef stew, rice, bread and coffee. I had a little bit of wine this noon. We fell in for detail at 1:30 P.M. to dig a hole to bury two horses that were killed by shrapnel while coming up to the Fort. Before they were cold, the cooks cut what meat was good and eatable, skinned it, and then got them ready for burial. We returned at 3:00 P.M. We fell in at 3:30 P.M. to 4:00 P.M. for school on automatic rifles. For mess we had steak mashed, bread and coffee. Orders came in to move tomorrow night. I wrote a letter to Aunt Hedwig, but they aren't collecting any more mail, so I will have to hold it until later.

The photo below of the two dead horses was taken by Charles W. Robertson and provided by Ellen (Asplund) Racine, curator of the Northborough Historical Society.

4-16-1918 Reveille was at 6:00 A.M. We policed up the quarters, then loaded the remaining five clips I carry. In all I am carrying 160 rounds of automatic ammunition and 100 rounds of rifle ammunition, quite a load! We were issued four boxes of hard bread and a can of hash for rations. Then I was detailed for wiring road frames with barbed wire which was finished about 10:30 A.M. It was raining and raw outside as we were preparing to leave. I rolled my pack and helped clean up the quarters. The boys say, "How we will miss this place!" A Company 103 Regiment will relieve us. The French officers inspected the quarters. For supper we had horse meat, bread, syrup and coffee.

4-17-1918 We left Liouville at 1:00 A.M. and hiked to Jouy until 5:00 A.M.. Some hike! Got to bed right away and up again at 10:00 A.M. Breakfast consisted of bread and coffee. We fell in at 12:00 and started to finish our march.

The weather was very muggy and the hiking was very muddy. This hike was one of the worst ones I've undertaken and I felt the most (about 29 kilometers). My legs were muscle bound and my feet were blistered. Some hike from Jouy and I was tired - whew! We arrived about 6:00 P.M. I went over to the Y.M.C.A. and got some cocoa, jam and cookies with my last bit of my change now gone. Our second mess for the day was hard bread and coffee at about 9:30 P.M. There was first class mail tonight. I received three letters from my Norma #34, #35, # 36, two from the Aldrich's, one from Carl O'Brien, and one from Arty Evans. I read all of these before going to bed at 12 P.M. God bless Norma dear. This place we are in now is Camp La Reharme. The nearest town is Menil-la-Tour.

4-18-1918 We got up about 9:30 A.M. Breakfast was much better today – rice, bacon, real punk and coffee. I reread my letters over again. The weather was fair but the walking sloppy. My legs are very sore, so I am resting this morning. We had only two meals today. At 4:30 P.M. I had the best dinner I've had in a long time: roast beef, mashed potatoes, gravy, cooked onions, bread, butter, figs and coffee. After this, I washed up and shaved. I sharpened a razor for Bates. I met Westy and Ned Fitzgerald this evening and had quite a talk with them. It was a pleasant evening. I made my bunk and will retire early. We are not more than five kilometers from the Front Lines.

4-19-1918 Patriot's Day. Reveille was at 6:30 A.M. We policed around the bunks. It is a very nice day. I did some sewing on my clothes this morning and sent the letter I previously wrote to Aunt Hedwig. I answered the letter to Etta Aldrich, Carl O'Brien, Arty Evans, and started letter #24 to Norma. During the afternoon, Abie, Jim, Westy, and Dave came over to see us from B.B. We went over to the range and tested our automatic rifles. Upon returning, I finished my letter to Norma. I sent it tonight. I had a very pleasant time today. I sent an "enemy" in the letter to Norma.

[I don't really know what the enemy he sent Norma was. I found many handkerchiefs and fancy post cards with fabric, all from France and one from Mexico, but none from Germany. He was picking flowers, pressing them and sending them to Norma. Perhaps he captured a dead bug (maybe a coocoo) from the caves and pressed it to send to Norma. When he was in New Mexico,

Walter skinned a large rattlesnake and sent the skin to her in a box along with some local cacti, an Indian doll, and a red sandstone peace pipe made by Native Americans.]

4-20-1918 There was a gas attack at 4:15 this morning. We kept our masks on until 6:00 A.M. We got up at 6:30 A.M. for mess and washed up. I went to see George Sheppard from the 102 M.G. Company. They suffered heavy losses and a lot of wounded and gas victims were returning from the Front Lines. Then we were ordered to roll our packs to move into the Front Lines again. We rested for the afternoon. We fell in for the march at 8:00 P.M. We had a gas alarm about 9:30 P.M. tonight. We were laying around in the streets awaiting the call to move forward. We found out we were only at a stand to, but it felt real. We were ready for anything to turn up, but it didn't come.

[I think the 102 M.G. Company means 102 machine gun company.)

4-21-1918. It was not until 3:00 A.M. in the morning that we had to turn in, but unfortunately, we lost our good sleeping quarters. We were put on the floor of the Y.M.C.A. to sleep. The place was a jam. It didn't take long before my head was pounding. I got up at 8:00 A.M. for coffee and bread. Then I came back and slept until 12:00 and got up for mess. We came back to our same places after dinner. The weather was fair, but it had rained early in the morning. George Sheppard came over and spent a few moments with me. We were talking over school days. The evening was spent peacefully. I retired early. It rained a little tonight.

4-22-1918 Reveille was at 7:00 A.M. It was a sloppy and muddy day. We cleaned up the barracks and had inspection of our equipment, gas masks, etc. At about 11:00 we went to Menil-la-Tour for a bath and had our clothes sterilized and laid around until they were done. On the way back, we were shelled – some fell several feet from us. I was put on detail for supper mess. We were gased – mustard gas is bad stuff! I received a very good letter #37 from Norma dated April 7, one from Norton's, one from Eddie, and one from Alice Reagan. There was a little entertainment tonight which was successful. Now I will retire for the night.

[Eddie is Walter's younger half-brother.]

4-23-1918 Reveille was at 7:00 A.M. I was detailed to help dig a hole where we dumped our rubbish. It was a sloppy day and this was a very sloppy duty although the weather was pleasant. In the afternoon I wrote some letters, one to father and the other to Alice Reagan. It's raining now pretty hard. I was put on detail to get water for the cook shack and laid around the rest of the day. I had it pretty much to myself which I appreciated. There was some entertainment tonight by the boys.

4-24-1918 Reveille was at 6:30 A.M. It was raining all day and very muddy. There were only a few details this morning; otherwise everything was all right. At noon we had a "wonderful" beef stew – ahem! with bread and coffee. About 3:00 P.M. this afternoon we were paid – I received one hundred eight-six francs. I gave Gene one hundred francs to keep for me. Then we were issued new underwear and stockings which were very much needed. A long needed change of underwear, believe me! We had a fair supper of beans, Jewish bread and coffee. Then Gene, H.S. and myself went to Menil-la-Tour about four kilometers from where we are at the present time. Gene bought a watch. I got some cocoa at the Salvation Army and bought some cookies. I came back to change my underwear before I retired. Things are very quiet tonight, so I wrote #41 letter to Norma.

[Gene is Walter's brother who was also in the 104th Infantry Regiment.]

4-25-1918 Reveille was at 6:30. Our platoon was on detail all morning. We emptied two rubbish cans. It was a rainy day and still very muddy. We played cards all afternoon and I made twenty francs! I was on gas sentry from 6:00 P.M. to 10:00 P.M. number 2 post. It was raining a little this evening. I retired after I came off guard duty.

4-26-1918 I got up at 5:30 A.M. and was on guard duty from 6:00 A.M. to 10:00 A.M. Then I went out with the Company on a working party with belts and rifles. It was a pleasant day today. We came back and rested until noon mess which consisted of pasty tomato stew, bread, prunes and coffee. Second class mail came in, but there was none for me. A "Norton Spirit" for March came in. For supper we had stew, peaches, dates, bread and coffee. I rolled the bones and made good. I passed the evening reading and thinking of my little girl back home. Nothing more important happened today, so I retired about 10:30 PM.

[The *Norton Spirit* is a monthly magazine published by Norton Company in Worcester, Massachusetts.]

[I think Walter meant they were playing dice when he said he rolled the bones.]

[According to bbc.com, the British government knew that mail was extremely important to keep up the morale of the soldiers. In Regent Park in London, a sorting office was set up in an extremely large wooden hut with a large staff consisting of women mainly to sort the mail by military unit. Every morning the bosses were informed of the latest movements of ships and battalions. A fleet of army lorries in Britain took the mail to Southampton or Folkestone to ships, where it was then shuttled over the ocean to depots called Army Postal Services located in Calais, Boulogne, or Le Havre in France. Trains took the mail at night from the French ports to the correct town to points where supplies for the divisions were to be transported. There were field post offices where regimental post orderlies would sort it and put it in carts, which they'd wheel to the front lines and deliver to the soldiers along with their meals. Letters from soldiers going back home were collected at the field post office after being censored, stamped with the field postmark, and then transported to the base post office. From there letters went to the train back to depots at the French ports to be shipped to Britain and from there to the U.S.][14]

4-27-1918 Reveille was at 5:30 A.M. After a breakfast of beef stew, bread and coffee, we prepared for a working party and fell in at 8:00 A.M. We hiked for some distance to a village nearer the Front Lines about 12 kilometers from Menil la Tour. We arrived in Toul about 8:45 A.M. We started to work on half hour reliefs digging a dugout for heavy bombardments. Walter provided the sketch below showing how the trench and dugout was constructed. The ground was very hard to dig in and very muddy. The weather was a peach and warm. We had oatmeal, syrup and plenty of water for lunch at noon. We worked again from 1:00 to 3:30 when we returned to our camp. We were ordered to clean and polish ourselves for the seventh day tomorrow. I had some appetite tonight!

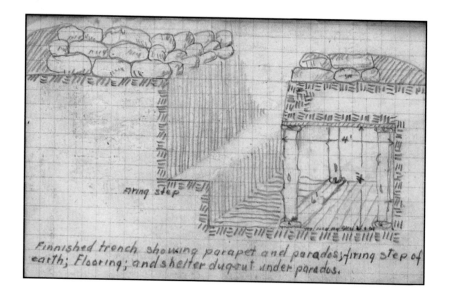

Finnished trench showing parapet and parados; firing step of earth; Flooring; and shelter dugout under parados.

4-28-1918 Sunday. Reveille was at 6:30 A.M. and we had oatmeal, bread and coffee for breakfast. We policed the barracks and laid around until 10:45 A.M. for mess of beef stew, bread and coffee. Then we fell in for the parade. During the first part of our journey, it started to rain. We were taken by truck to a field near Boucq. Then we marched to the top of a large hill where we were met by General Clarence G. Edwards, quite a gathering. Ours was the first American regiment to be decorated for their valor with the war cross by the French, called the Croix de Guerre. We returned by truck to our barracks. I took a hike to Royaumeix, then to Menil-la-Tour and back to our barracks. It was 10:30 P.M. by that time. I got a dozen of eggs for six francs. I came back soaking wet from the rain. I slept very well this night.

I think the following photo of Walter was taken at this gathering.

[According to Wikipedia, the 104th infantry was cited for its gallantry by order of the French 32nd Army Corps. The infantry's regimental flag was decorated with the Croix de Guerre (i.e. war cross) by French General Fenelon F.G. Passaga. This was the first American unit honored by a foreign country for exceptional bravery in combat. During the same ceremony, 117 members of the 104th infantry along with its commander, Colonel George H. Shelton received the award.][15]

[As Walter stated above, he was present there. I believe he has a cross medal on his uniform in his photo on the book cover.]

4-29-1918 Reveille was at 6:30 A.M. Breakfast at 7:00 was bacon, spuds, bread and coffee. With this I cooked up half a dozen eggs. This was the first real breakfast I've had since I came to France. It is raining today. There was not much doing this morning, so we played cards. They are not taking any mail. Pop Vincent goes back to cooking today. This afternoon we played cards and I came out good. This afternoon cleared up a bit with the sun shining. After a very good supper of beans, bread, bread pudding, and coffee, we went back to playing cards until 11:30. I received a letter from Frenchy dated April 3, 1918. Then I retired.

4-30-1918 Reveille was at 6:30 A.M. We policed around the barracks. I cleaned my rifle. There was a muster for pay this morning from 9:00 to 10:30 A.M. We played cards until 12:30 P.M. I rolled the bones this afternoon. Conte and myself went for a walk this afternoon to a town named Minouville, where we had a swell feed and a good time. It rained this afternoon. I bought cheese for five francs a pound – some cheese! We returned about 10:30 P.M. I got a paper from my girl. Simmons borrowed ten francs from me.

5-1-1918 Reveille was at 6:30 A.M. I rolled my pack and got ready to leave. We expect to leave before tomorrow. We cleaned and policed up the entire barracks. There was such a dirty mess under the bunks left by the last bunch. We played cards until dinner which was at 2:00 P.M. We played cards again until 3:00 P.M. Then we fell in for our hike. It was a really hot and muggy day to hike and we were so sweaty – whew! It was about 11:00 P.M. before we got settled in this town of Broussey-Raulecourt. We got a fair place to sleep. I was pretty tired after our march. We relieved the 101st Regiment. I got some nuts, biscuits, candy and pinot noir (French wine). On this hike I never saw so many forget-me-nots. They were all along the roadside. It put me in mind of the past back home.

[Broussey-Raulecourt is in the Meuse department in Grand Est in Lorraine in northeastern France. His words toward the end here made me realize how very homesick Walter was all through his service in France. His friends and family were always extremely important to him and he loved his home in the Worcester area.]

5-2-1918 There was no reveille this morning so I got up about 8:30 A.M. I got a pair of rubber boots. After this, I went down and cleaned up. It is a peach of a day and very quiet. I went to the band concert given by the 101st Regiment Band. This is the first band I have heard since my arrival in France. I rested the remainder of the afternoon. It was a glorious day all the way through. I rolled my pack and got ready to leave here to move nearer the Front Lines. We left here on the ammunition wagons at about 9:00 P.M. and it was an all night affair. It got quite chilly around midnight. We had quite a layover.

5-3-1918 We got to the Front Lines about 4:30 A.M. I hiked with 3 clip bags, a pair of shoes and boots, my pack, a belt with 100 rounds, 360 rounds of automatic ammunition, an overcoat, and gas masks. This was some load to carry! I was all in when we struck the place. Our Company is going into the Front Lines right away with no rest. We had our breakfast mess about 8:00 A.M. It was a peach of a day. I picked up my bed and have found a better place. This place is knocked for a goal, so we have a long stand-to - it's dangerous for a flank attack here. There are lots of anti-aircraft shots today. I slept this afternoon until mess at 5:00 P.M. I cleaned my rifle and clips for tonight. We were in the Front Line trenches at 9:00 P.M. It was a quiet night in our sector. I slept on boxes of bombs, etc. with somewhat disquieting thoughts, but I slept just the same for one hour.

[Walter gave a list of armaments and equipment (French system) with weights:

a.	Gunner	
	Pouch with pistol and 3 clips	2.9 lbs
	Gun with sheath	20 lbs.
	Clip pouches (4 clips)	8.8 lbs.
	Belt	.9 lb.
	Bag with 4 clips & cleaning kit	10.3 lbs.
b.	1st Carrier	
	Pouch with pistol and 3 clips	2.9 lbs.

Haversack with 8 clips and cartridge packet	24.0 lbs.
Bag with 4 cartridge packets	17.9 lbs.
Belt	.9 lb.

c. 2nd Carrier

Rifle and equipment with one packet distributed in the cartridge pouches

Haversack with 5 packets and 4 clips

(This is the French way)

Cartridges carried:

Gunner	160 rds.
1st Carrier	480 rds.
2nd Carrier	400 rds.
" " 100 rds. Of .30 Springfield Am extra	]

5-4-1918 I was up all morning. It was quite a strain looking out on No Man's Land. I returned to the rear of our company, although we are still in the Front Lines just the same. This was at 5:00 A.M. Breakfast mess was at 6:30 and consisted of bacon, spuds, bread and coffee. There's mud up to our knees in these trenches - some mud and water! It was a peach of a day. The swallows came into their ruined homes – they are very tame. They don't seem to mind the noise. I slept all the rest of the morning and part of the afternoon. I got up and cleaned my rifle and automatic clips again for tonight. Mess at 6:00 P.M. was the same as last night: hash only with no bread, beans instead. We fell in at 8:30 P.M. for the Front Line. They brought us coffee about 12:30 at night. It is quiet tonight. There were flare lights from the Germans mostly. We expected something??

5-5-1918 We came back to the rear about 5:00 A.M. and cleaned the mud off of our boots and then went to breakfast mess. The weather was undecided – it may rain. I'm getting a bad cold in my chest from standing in the mud and water up to my knees. I will turn in for some sleep. There was a big barrage on our left this morning about 8:30 A.M. The big guns from our side were doing fine work. I woke up at 12:30 P.M. and shared a can of salmon with Charlie. Then we went back to sleep. Shells were bursting all around this town which woke me up about 3:30 P.M. It rained continuously this afternoon. Supper mess was a beef stew with Jewish bread, rice pudding and coffee. I'm getting ready to hit the Front Line in the trenches tonight at 8:30 P.M. It's some sloppy mess tonight – I'm soaked to the skin. I carried stones to fill in the muddiest part of our trench. I knocked off work at 12:00 at night.

Walter provided more sketches of the how the trenches were constructed.

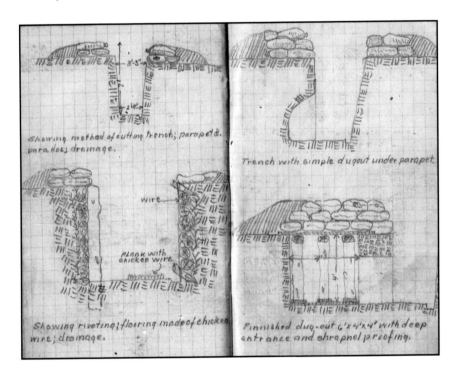

5-6-1918 It rained all night and morning. There was a heavy barrage on our right at about 3:00 A.M. this morning. REAL LIFE and SOME SIGHT! They very nearly opened up fire on our own men in No Man's Land and we aren't getting any word if they were still out there. I left the Front Line at 5:00 A.M. We had to wait for mess this morning and it was some wait! We didn't know whether we were going to get it or not - some system! We had had coffee about 1:00 during the night. It cleared up a bit this morning about 5 A.M. Gene went up to the neck in mud and water last night. We worked all night and slept day. The mail came in, but as yet none for me. I got up at 3:00 P.M. I cleaned my two rifles, shaved and cleaned up myself. I hit the trenches at 8:30 tonight. There were a few changes in our positions - a few mix-ups tonight.

[In Clarence Nelson's diary, he related that two dead soldiers from the 101st infantry were brought in today. They had been on a party of five fixing wire when they ran into an enemy patrol. The other three were captured. There were U.S. soldiers holding a destroyed village out in No Man's Land during the daytime. At night a German machine gunner was in the village raking the U.S. trenches. Clarence related many incidences when he and other soldiers went out on patrol and fired on Germans and were fired on by the Germans. This information was provided courtesy of Ellen (Asplund) Racine, curator at the Northborough Historical Society.]

5-7-1918. Father's Birthday We had coffee at 1:30 A.M. I was relieved for one hour. Watchful waiting! A few patrols were out this morning. There was no rain tonight – I was thankful for this. A few shots were fired in our vicinity this morning. I returned from the Front Lines about 5:00 A.M. While eating breakfast, I was handed two letters – one from Norma and one from Helen Sawyer. It was a pleasant day today. Now for some sleep. The "Stars and Stripes" came this morning which I read before retiring. I started a letter to Norma, but felt too tired to finish it, so I went to sleep. I woke up at 12:30 and finished #25 letter to Norma. Then I had some French hard tack. There was a terrific thunderstorm raging and it rained all evening, so that I was soaked to the skin. There was shelling fifty to seventy-five yards in our rear – some were close ones. This was the worst night I've spent in the trenches.

[Besides shelling from bombs and shrapnel bursting all over the place, they were being targeted by a German machine gunner raking their trenches. The enemy sent up flares so they could see where the U.S. troops happened to be. I have been so impressed with Walter's diary and how he mentioned all the holidays and remembered everybody's birthday when he was in the midst of all this horror and had to stay alert in order not to lose his life or allow the enemy to sneak in and harm his fellow soldiers. It's a real tribute to the caring type of person he happened to be throughout his entire life.]

5-8-1918 It rained all morning. It was a very dark night. I didn't sleep all night or morning. The trenches were filled with mud and water – some experience, believe me! I returned from the trenches at 5:00 A.M. and was drenched to the skin with mud up to my neck. My rifle was a sight and my automatic clips were all mud. Our Company was covering a battalion front, and it was some job! After I got back at 4:00 P.M, I slept all morning and afternoon. For mess we had tomato soup, hard bread and coffee. Afterwards, I cleaned my rifle and automatic clips for the lines at 8:30 P.M. It was a very dark night and a very shaky night with a lot of bombing and shrapnel bursting all over the place. I felt as if something was coming at any moment! Two patrols were out. However, to my knowledge there weren't any casualties in our Companies.

5-9-1918 Coffee came about 12:30 A.M. It was an icky night all through. There were numerous shots, bombs, and machine guns working. It sounded like rifles, automatic rifles, and rifle grenades all being fired at once with flashes all over. What a confusing time! Every one of us was all nerved up! We came back to the rear at 5:00 A.M. Since mess wasn't until 7:00 A.M, we hung around discussing the night's experience until it did come. I slept but very little about three hours. I got up for detail to police the town, for we are leaving tonight. I got packed and ready to move to the rear. 2nd battalion H Company came in tonight. It's very foggy tonight. This place we are in is Xivray. We went in the lines and on our way in we got a reception going in. Machine gun fire was sweeping our lines, so we had to keep down.

[In Clarence Nelson's diary, he recounted that a divisional order came in for fifty men and two lieutenants from A and C Companies to raid the German sector to the west of their position out in No Man's Land. On the patrol, they ran into an enemy patrol who opened fire on them. One of the lieutenants shouted to his patrol to "Give it to 'em, boys," which is exactly what they did with rifles, automatic rifles, pistols, and rifle grenades. Nelson reported that bullets were hitting all around the group and the Germans withdrew. Only one member of their team was wounded. This was a confusing time that Walter and the other men on guard saw and heard which is why they were all nerved up. This information was provided courtesy of Ellen (Asplund) Racine, curator of the Northborough Historical Society.]

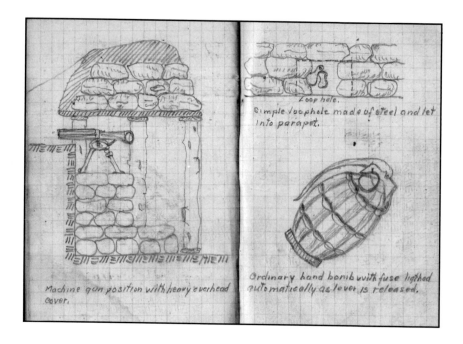

Machine gun position with heavy overhead cover.

Loop hole.
Simple loophole made of steel and let into parapet.

Ordinary hand bomb with fuse lighted automatically as lever is released.

5-10-1918 I was relieved at 2:00 A.M. this morning. Corporal Lowell's gun team relieved us. This was the first time I've met him since we were at Westfield. We left this place at 3:00 A.M. for our hike to the rear. We came back through Raulecourt about two kilometers to the rear of this, in a large woods and billeted here. We got here about 6:00 A.M. I was pretty tired as I had only about two and one-half hours of sleep since yesterday at 2:00 P.M. I slept until noon mess which was about 11:30 A.M. I got some goodies at the Y.M.C.A. I feel tired but am restless. I wrote to Ma Kjellberg, a letter for Mother's Day, and Irving French rather than eating noon mess. For supper we had cornwilly, mashed spuds, bread and coffee. My bunkie brought my mess to my bunk. I went to bed quite late at 12:20.

[I am so impressed by his ability to draw the cross sections of how the trenches were constructed and set up. I know he was an artist, but it appears he was also a draftsman and engineer. I say this from my experience in drawing plans for my husband and our construction company.]

5-11-1918 Reveille was at 7:00 A.M. I sharpened a number of razor blades for the boys and shaved myself and cleaned up. I cleaned up my rifle and equipment a bit. It's a very nice day. There were only a few details this morning, such as policing, etc. At 3:00 P.M. we had inspection of our rifles and equipment. I passed OK. We had another detail of policing and cleaning up around the barracks. I went for a swim this afternoon – the first of the season. I wrote to the Hall's thanking them for the box they sent me today, including sardines and candy. I got a carton of cigarettes from Irving today. I sent a letter answering Helen Sawyer's of April 6th. We had a heavy rainstorm at 6:30 P.M. while we were at mess. We went to the movies at the Y.M.C.A. I retired about 12 P.M.

5-12-1918 Mother's Day. At 3:00 A.M. I was hauled out of bed in the middle of my sleep for a bath. I was some disgusted – it got my goat! Especially after yesterday's bath. This got everybody's goat for that matter. We hiked to Roulecourt for the bath and had our clothes sterilized from the crumbs. [It is near Xivray which is in the northeast of France near Lorraine.] Our blankets also went through the same process. I bought a dozen of eggs and had a feed to my own taste – cooked it myself. The weather is disagreeable today. I wrote to Jack and Mr. and Mrs. Eggleston. I didn't want mess but ate a bunch of nuts and cookies and chocolate. I was detailed to dig two straddle trenches. This was some job digging in the mud. I wrote #26 letter to Norma.

5-13-1918 Reveille was at 7:00 A.M. There were a few details this morning. After I finished my morning's work, I laid down and snoozed until it was time for dinner. Afterwards, we had a detail to police around the barracks for sanitation purposes. Then I went for a walk in the woods and picked a bunch of wild Lilies of the Valley. When I returned, I had a letter from Norma, #40 dated April 22. I had a peculiar feeling as I was returning – I felt that the letter was coming. After supper, I was paid one hundred eighty-six francs for two months. I went broke today – no luck playing poker. It's a very dark night tonight, looks like rain before morning.

5-14-1918 Reveille was at 7:00 A.M. We policed around our bunks. We were then detailed all morning cleaning up the place, digging holes and one thing or another. The afternoon was spent on details. I had a short rest. It was a very nice afternoon – I laid out in the sun. For supper we had flapjacks and coffee. It tasted very good for a change. I was detailed to carry water from the tank to the kitchen. Today was a strenuous day. This evening we played cards. At 12:00 I was on guard for four hours. We had a moonlight night. Charlie did his guard tonight and took an A.W.O.L.

5-15-1918 About 3:00 A.M. there was a heavy barrage on our left. I heard machine guns from here. The big gun in our rear was pounding. When she fires, it shakes our barracks some. It's a naval gun. Airplanes were reconnoitering overhead. I came off guard at 4:30 A.M. after being up all night. I slept until breakfast mess. I had to get up and fold my blankets – there was little rest for me. It is a beautiful day and warm today. I went for a walk in the woods and was outside all afternoon enjoying the air. I enjoyed the evening but had a bad headache - playing cards did it no doubt. There's not much doing so far, it's quiet.

[Reconnoitering was an exploratory military survey of enemy territory.]

5-16-1918 Reveille was at 7:00 A.M.. I policed around the bunks, cleaned up a bit and folded my blankets. At 9:30 A.M. we had a formation of patrol executions for No Man's Land: horseshoe, arrow and diamond formations. It was a very important instruction. We were dismissed to wash our clothes. It was a beautiful day, a wonderful day. At 1:00 P.M. we fell in for inspection and were dismissed until 2:00 P.M. We had a maneuver through the woods, acted as an ambush, against a platoon as patrol. It was very well instructed. We returned at 5:00 P.M.. I received a very nice letter #39 from Norma and one from Mrs. F.H. Lucke. We played cards until 10:00 P.M.. First I sewed my pants and then I sewed on my service stripe for six months service. Following this I wrote in my diary. This finished the day's events.

Walter's sketches about battle formations are below:

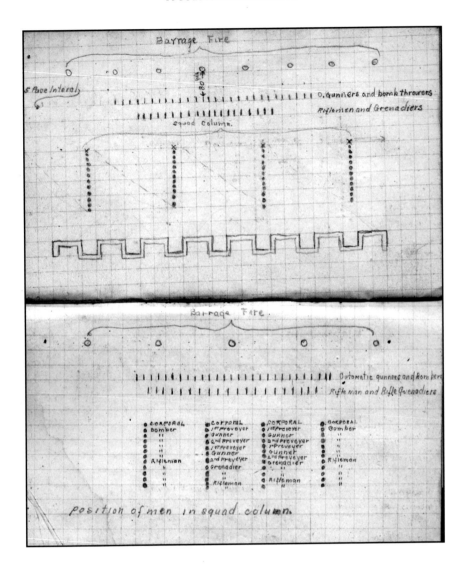

5-17-1918 Reveille was at 7:00 A.M.. We policed around the barracks, shaved and cleaned up. Silently, we walked out to a card game. There were no results this morning. It was a beautiful and very peaceful morning. There were a few buss planes hovering in the air. After dinner, there was plenty to do: we rolled our packs for our next place nearer the Front Lines. There were plenty of details to perform, such as cleaning up the camp. We played cards to pass the time along. We did our final cleaning up. Five American girls came to the

Y.M.C.A. for an entertainment. It was splendid and a great feeling to see a real American girl, believe me! I'm lonesome for Norma, my girl. We started our hike at 9:00 P.M. and got to Brussey about 10:30 P.M.. We are in support here.

[Brussey is in the township of Marnay, which is part of the district of Vesoul in the department of Haute-Saone in the French region of Franche-Comte in east France.]

5-18-1918 We got up about 8:00 A.M.. It was another beautiful day. It looks like a peaceful place, quite a large town. There are a number of planes reconnoitering the lines today. I laid out in the shade this morning. The afternoon was the same as this morning, warm, peaceful and quiet around here. The birds are very peaceful, singing and contented, although there is some noise from the guns. There was a rain shower while I was sleeping which woke me up, so I beat it to my bunk. I am in a very good place with Charlie my Bunkie. After supper, we played a few hands of cards, until almost 10:00 P.M.. When the mail came in, I received four letters which made me feel good, one from Norma, one from John Kjellberg, one from Pratt and one from A.E. Reagan. I am a happy boy tonight. I will now retire, closing my day's work and thoughts.

[Walter didn't mention when Charlie came back after going A.W.O.L., but I think it's the same Charlie.]

5-19-1918 I arose at 10:00 A.M.. It was another beautiful day today, peaceful and quiet. I did not eat breakfast this morning. Rather, I went to the washroom to wash up and shave. There are hundreds of birds around here singing their many notes, mostly swallows. Last night I managed to pick up a tame one. This morning I wrote a letter to Pa Kjellberg. During the afternoon, I wrote letter #27 to Norma. I received a very nice letter # 41 from Norma today. I also wrote to father today and sent him three designs [his father designed wallpaper in a factory in Worcester, Massachusetts, and Walter was also an artist.] About 5:00 P.M. we had a thunderstorm which didn't last very long. Things are very quiet here tonight and I feel very blue. From 8:00 to 12:00 P.M. I was on detail, helping the Engineers load lumber and material for dug outs, etc.

5-20-1918 I got to bed at 1:30 A.M. this morning – it was a beautiful moonlight night. I slept until 8:00 A.M.. It is another beautiful, warm day. This morning I got ten rusty clips which I cleaned up, as well as my rifle. We had a formation this morning to see who had shot on the ranges and who hadn't. According to reports, we go into the Front Lines soon, so I am ready to move tomorrow. We had a very good dinner of roast beef hash, seasoning, mashed potatoes, bread and coffee. My afternoon was "spent" with Norma, writing #28 letter to answer her #41 letter to me. I was laying out in the open. I sent Norma's letter along with the one I wrote to Mr. Kjellberg yesterday and three pressed flowers I had picked: lily of the valley, forget me nots and daisies. After this, I had a nap. Since there was not much of anything doing tonight, I went to bed early.

5-21-1918 We arose at 8:00 A.M.. After breakfast I shaved and cleaned up. We are getting things ready to move tonight. It is another beautiful day and rather quiet. I saw many airplanes in the air this morning. I was issued a spoon and fork this morning. After dinner, I rolled my pack and am ready to leave anytime. Upon finishing, I came out under the nearby apple tree and laid down to sleep until 4:30 P.M.. For supper, we had a very tasty hash, bread and coffee. I went on guard from 6 to 9 P.M.. It was a beautiful moonlight night, so I wrote these lines by moonlight around 10:00 P.M. . I was relieved about 10:30 by I Company of 104th Regiment. We marched about eight kilometers tonight which lasted until early the next morning. We went through some terrible Front Line trenches with mud and water over our shoe tops. It was a moonlight night. The password to get through the trenches was Danker-Denton (in symbols).

5-22-1918 We relieved E Company of 102nd Regiment at about 3:30 this morning. I had an accident this morning: unfortunately, I took a spill in the mud and went in all over. I was a terrible sight. Did I cuss – well you guess! We are about five hundred yards from the German lines, the worst Front Lines our Company has been in to date. I was up all night, didn't get settled until about 6:00 A.M.. Then we went in our dugout we had made to get some sleep. The sun was very hot today, so it was uncomfortable sleeping. After bread and coffee mess at 10:00 A.M., I went down to a shell hole and washed myself, trying to clean off some of the mud I had collected on my clothes, etc. when I fell. We are on the right of Xivray where we were some time ago. This position is much better for us to attack from than our previous one at Xivray (Xivray-et-Marvoisin). Our many "friends" are with us: rats. The gun team I'm in has got a post out in the second line of wire in No Mans Land. I slept one and one-half hours out there, during my relief, with plenty of mosquitos.

Walter's sketch below shows positions of advance guard work and also simple cover showing use of sand bags.

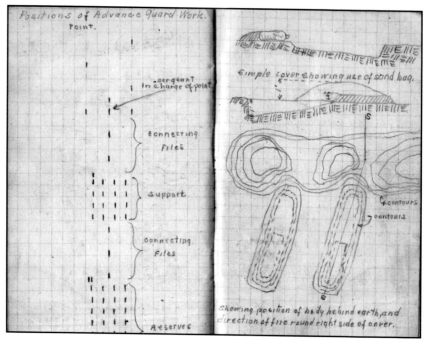

5-23-1918 We returned at 3:30 A.M. and stand to was until 5:00 A.M.. We policed our sector of the trench. It is another beautiful day. There are many observation balloons up today. I went on guard for one hour from 11 A.M. to 12:00. A box from Norma came to me in the trenches with peanuts, raisins and fudge which came in very handy. It was very thoughtful of Norma putting in some raisins. I awoke to a coming storm and made the best preparations I could to keep what rain I could out of my roofless dugout. I got it just about covered and down came the rain. Whew! Was I soaked! Our supper was bacon, spuds, beans, bread and coffee. Although everything was muddy, this didn't stop us from eating it. Stand to was in the trenches from 8:00 to 9:30 P.M.. Then we took our same post as yesterday. Password: Naravon, check Nelson (in symbols). It's quieter tonight from previous nights.

5-24-1918 I returned from my post at 3:00 A.M.. Stand to was from 3 to 5:00 A.M.. I policed around my dugout and drained off the water settling in the trenches. It is a beautiful day today. I slept from 10:00 to 11:00 and then went on guard until 12:00. I slept until 4:00 P.M.. The supper of bacon, mashed spuds, raisins, syrup, bread and coffee was the best feed we've had since arriving here this time. It rained pitch forks in the afternoon, and off and on during the evening. I started work from 8 to 9:30 and then went out to my post. I slept two hours when on relief at my post. It was a raw cold night. There were three parties out looking for trouble, but didn't get any. The password was Soissl, check, Scully (in symbols). It was another quiet evening. It was a good night for a raid, but there weren't any.

5-25-1918 I returned from my post at 3:15 A.M.. I slept in the trench until 5:00 A.M.. It's a quiet morning and a good day. The birds are whistling their many tunes. I came back to my dugout and policed around the place. I turned in until mess came at about 9:30 A.M. It's a beautiful day, so I stayed up and witnessed an airplane shot down while hovering over the Boche lines. At 10:30 A.M. there were several shells passing overhead. After this occurrence, General Cole came through and balled me out for not wearing my gas mask at alert. I cleaned up and shaved and sharpened a razor for Pendergast. I will get some sleep for later. Charlie had cramps, so I didn't get much chance to sleep. I got some salts for the kid at B.H. I went on stand to from 8:00 to 9:30 P.M. and then out to my post. I distinctly heard the Boche ripping apart the plane that they plugged at and also heard them put it on the trucks. Then they sped away. This was on our right. The password was Madere, check Magellan (in symbols).

5-26-1918 I returned from the outpost at 3:30 A.M.. Then we had stand to in the trench until 5:00 A.M.. During stand to, a sniper from the German side was having a good time shooting a few of them over at us. One passed pretty close to me while I was writing this line. I policed the section of the trenches I'm assigned to. This morning it's a fair day but chilly. I turned in about 6:00 A.M. until mess of bacon, spuds, bread and coffee. After mess, I turned back to bed again (what I now call it) – I slept on two duck boards. It turned out to be a beautiful day and rather quiet in the lines. I wrote #29 letter to Norma, four pages long. With it, I sent a poppy that I found in the lines. There are quite a number of poppies around here. Stand to was from 8:00 to 9:30 P.M.. Following that, I went way out on Nobody's Property on a patrol with our rifles, shot it and returned to the same post as the other nights. The password was aspaiyn – astain (in symbols). It is a moonlight night, but a there's a heavy dew on the ground.

5-27-1918 The password was suez – suffreu (in symbols). At 2:00 A.M. this morning there was a heavy bombardment on our right. Fifteen minutes later we called for a heavy barrage in front of our lines, the heaviest I've experienced in the lines. For the first few minutes, I was a bit nervous but got over it later. The purpose of this barrage in our front was a precautionary measure in case of them overlapping or flanking us. It was a hot time, believe me! It took two minutes as we withdrew from the outpost where the Boche were shelling the spot we laid in. Without the machine guns, one pounders, 75's, and big guns in our rear, there wouldn't have been any chance for us at all. Then the Boche put a few gas shells mixed in with the other shells. With the wind in their favor, it kind of made us sit up and take notice. It was a beautiful day. Stand to was from 8:00 to 9:30. We couldn't go out to our post, because we were being held back by machine guns sweeping the trench. I guess they (the Boche) got hip to our position - maybe their purpose was holding us back here.

5-28-1918 There was a good deal of shell fire last night and this morning. Machine guns were sweeping our trench all night and morning. One gas shell hit nearby which made us put on our gas masks. This was a leery night, watchful, waiting for what might have turned up. This is getting to be a noisy sector since we came here. They were playing with minenwerfers on our front most lines. Stand to was 3 to 4:30 this morning. I came back then and retired until breakfast mess of bacon, spuds, bread and coffee. It was a beautiful day on the coast. The Boche shelled the daylights out of the town in our rear at 5:00 A.M.. There's a good range on their guns. I slept until 4:30 P.M. when supper of beans, cornwilly hash, bread and coffee came. Pendergast leaves us today for the Headquarters Platoon. Stand to was from 8 to 9:30 P.M. Then we crawled on our hands and knees to our position. It was no easy task. We had to withdraw from our position fifteen minutes later. A Boche sniper was having a great time again tonight. They opened up with machine guns. It was a moonlight night again. Password to get through the trenches was Belfort – bara (in symbols).

[*Minenwerfer* is the German name for a sort of range mortar. They were used to clear obstacles like bunkers and barbed wire.]

5-29-1918 There was quite a lot of shelling this morning by the Boche in the surrounding towns. It's another good day so far, but not promising as it's pretty cloudy today. This morning I was issued a new pair of socks which I badly needed. Clothing is very hard to get some way or other. After waking up from my sleep and after stand to, the mail arrived and I received two letters from Norma #42 and #43, dated April 29 and May 5, one from E. Johnson, and one from Norton's. This put new life into me since I've been in this sector. Then I went back for my final sleep of the day until mess time. About this time we saw a red balloon up in the air which came down in front of our second line of wire. Gene went out on his hands and knees looking for it, but came back without it. The Boche took a few shots at him when he was out there. I shaved and washed up getting ready for tonight's duty. Password: ropefort – reslieu (in symbols). It was a much quieter night for us. Stand to was from 8:00 to 9:30 P.M. and then we worked in reliefs throughout the night. (Dentcher ballon, kann vernichtet werdern).

[The translation to the German words above is "German balloons can be destroyed."]

5-30-1918 Decoration Day (or Memorial Day). There was not much doing this morning. Only once in a while there was an "Artillery Duel". This morning was a bit chilly. Stand to was from 3 to 5:00 A.M. It's going to be a beautiful day today. I turned in for some sleep until mess came. How cheerful it is to hear the birds singing in the early morning hours at daybreak, one of our most watchful moments. I went on duty as gas and observation guard in the trench from 11 to 12:30 A.M. Afterwards I went back to rest until 3:00 P.M. I was detailed to get the mess for supper. This is some job and some hike through the trenches! The supper of roast beef, potatoes, bread and coffee was very good for once. I rolled my pack and am ready to haul out when the bombardment starts. Tonight we are pulling off a raid in front of our lines. We are watchfully waiting from stand to until the time the bombardment starts. It's a noisy sector for the time. I lugged plenty of ammunition in from P.C. quite a ways from my post. There was a short barrage from offensive so we pulled out of the trenches at that time.

[Walter is receiving some kind of commendation in the photo below, but I don't know what it was for. I think he received a Croix de Guerre on April 28, 1918. I think you can see it on his uniform in the photo on the cover. Sometime after he was wounded on July 20, 1918, he did receive a purple heart, which I have in my possession – maybe this was what he received in this photo.]

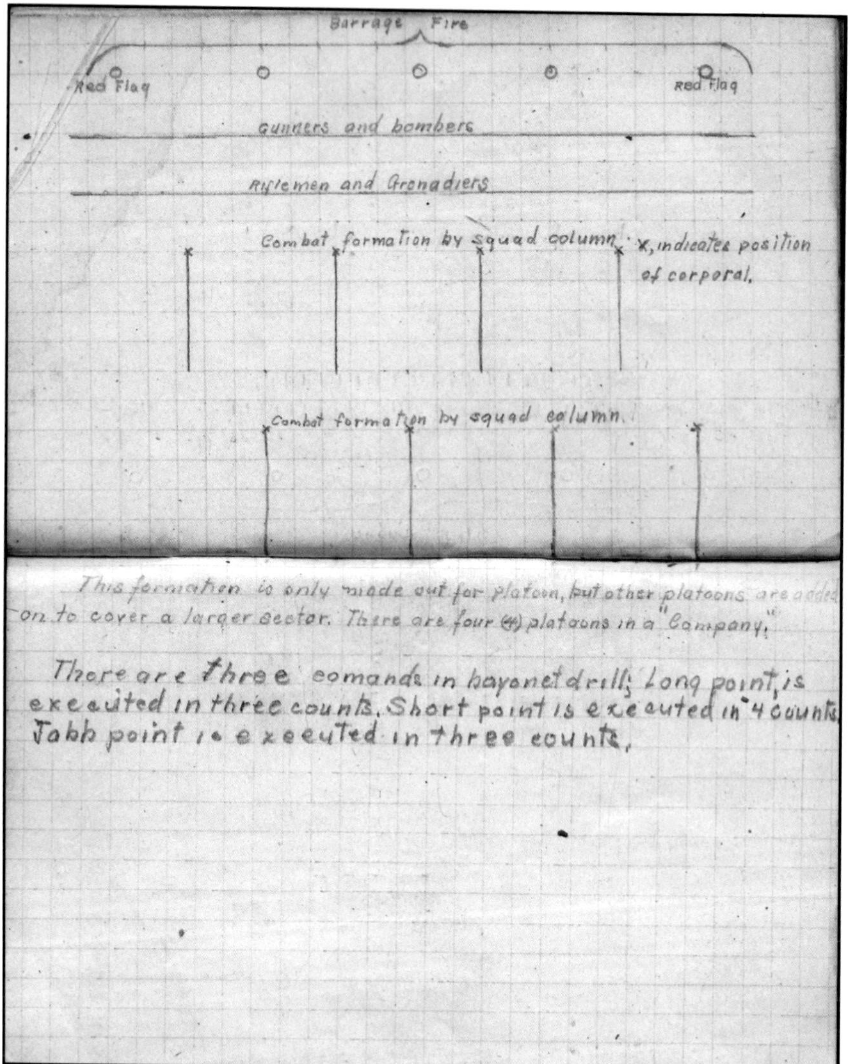

Barrage Fire

Red Flag   O   O   O   Red Flag

Gunners and bombers

Riflemen and Grenadiers

Combat formation by squad column. x, indicates position of corporal.

Combat formation by squad column.

This formation is only made out for platoon, but other platoons are added on to cover a larger sector. There are four (4) platoons in a "Company."

There are three comands in bayonet drill; Long point, is executed in three counts. Short point is executed in 4 counts. Jabb point is executed in three counts.

Walter's sketch above shows the combat formation for platoons. He notes that there are four platoons in a Company.

5-31-1918 Our company got to Beaumont at about 2:30 and dug for the cave here. It was quite a hike to get here and talk about the mud and water we went through to get here! I was soaked through and very nearly took a spill again. The cave was terribly wet and muddy within, but well protected from shells. Our heavy bombardment started at 2:45 A.M. and lasted about one hour. There was a roar of a hundred guns in one chorus and shells were sent into Germany, covering every enemy position. Every 16 inch shell made a roar like a train of cars. There sure was some noise! I laid down to sleep and got up about 7:30 this morning. For breakfast we had cornwilly sandwiches and coffee. I went to the Y.M.C.A. and got chocolate and cookies. When I returned back to the Front Lines again, I found things the same as when I left. I laid out my things and rested rather than slept. When I woke up, I had received four letters – from Erhard, Arty Evans, Kate Manning, and Leopold Rudolph. Stand to was from 8 to 9:30 P.M. and I worked in reliefs. It's rather peaceful tonight – a nice evening. There was a new barrage on a different position. The password was suzzey – sircourt (in symbols).

6-1-1918 Stand to was from 3 to 5 A.M. Then I came back to my bunk to sleep. It is a beautiful day. Things are quiet – more so than before. I received a letter from Mrs. Reagan with a bunch of pictures. After mess, I went back to dreams until 11:00. Guard duty was from 11:00 A.M. to 12:00. I tried to sleep after guard duty, but it was so hot and muggy that I was just able to rest. Stand to was from 8:00 to 9:30 P.M. and I took my old position again on account of the 4th Platoon moving out. We went on patrol out in front and shot up flares through the bombs and automatic rifles. We then returned to our posts. It was a rather warm and peaceful night. We worked in two-hour reliefs. I had first relief. There was a sniper on the enemy side working tonight, sweeping the trenches.

6-2-1918 Stand to was from 3 to 5:00 A.M. After that I came back and laid down. It was a rather quiet and beautiful morning. I slept until breakfast mess and went on guard from 10 to 11:00 A.M. In the meanwhile, I shaved and cleaned up, making preparations to withdraw from the Front Lines. The 2nd Battalion is to relieve us tonight. We have been quite fortunate with the weather, only one day was bad. We were in the Front Lines for twelve days and there wasn't one casualty, still a horseshoe with us I guess [i.e. lucky break]. Stand to was from 8 to 9:30 P.M.. We worked in reliefs. We rolled our packs and got ready to leave. It is a rather warm and quiet evening. H Company relieves us tonight.

[When Walter says "still a horseshoe with us," he's referring to the many times his company has been bombed but nobody has been killed. Sergeant Clarence Nelson said nearly the same thing in his diary quite a few times.]

6-3-1918 I was relieved about 1:30 A.M. On our way out we were shelled. They sure did get the beat on us! There seems to be a great spying system going on in these parts. We all got out safely and passed through Ramecourt to Roulecourt, where we are now stationed. We arrived here about 3:30 A.M. I took sick suddenly this morning. I guess it's the trench fever, a very disagreeable feeling. I laid in the bunk all day. The weather was beautiful and warm. This afternoon I was issued underwear and stockings.

6-4-1918 I was pretty weak this morning. Charlie brought my breakfast this morning. I got up for sick call. It's a beautiful day. Breakfast was rice, applesauce, doughnuts, bread and coffee. It was very good. I laid down all morning, feeling pretty weak from the effects of the trench fever. During the afternoon, I went out in the shade and slept until it was time for supper mess of roast beef, mashed spuds, bread and coffee. At 10:00 P.M. we went to the positions and returned about 11:30 P.M. It was very peaceful on the Front Lines.

6-5-1918 I got up at 8:00 A.M. I went out for a walk through the fields and saw many different flowers from those at home. There seems to be many poppies in these parts. It is a glorious summer's day and I enjoyed it very much. I came to a pond that put me in mind of the lake at home so much. For dinner we had beans, bread and coffee. To go with this I bought some mustard and milk at a French canteen. After dinner, I took my blanket outside and spent the time writing #30 letter to my Norma. I sent my service stripe and a poppy along with the four pages. We went through a gas test in the chamber with two Salvation Army girls. This evening we went to the entertainment at the Y.M.C.A. which we enjoyed. At 10 bells I went on guard at the Colonel's Headquarters. I was relieved about 1:00 A.M. I had a mean fall right on my right crazy bone and bled like a stuck pig.

6-6-1918 I was relieved about 1:00 A.M. and went up to the hospital where they bandaged me. I came back and slept until 4:00 A.M. and then stood guard until eight bells. Breakfast was very different: bread pudding, rice pudding, bread and coffee. It's another glorious day. Because I didn't have much sleep last night, I slept all morning. I received a new box respirator, as my old one was condemned. For dinner we got roast beef, mashed spuds, gravy, bread pudding and coffee. I bought some sweet corn which went great with it. I slept all afternoon. I drank quite a lot of rouge today (red wine?). For supper they served beef stew, bread and coffee. Instead I bought some beans, heated them up, and had some strong mustard with them. Gene goes to the hospital today. It seems everybody is infected with the trench fever. I got my dose and know what it's like. They are a pretty quiet bunch tonight. I haven't had much time to do any letter writing. I slept fairly well tonight.

6-7-1918 I got up at 8:00 A.M. It's another glorious day. We have a pretty sick bunch of boys this morning. I went out in the shade and started a letter to Erhard #3. I enjoyed a good dinner today of steak, mashed potatoes, jam, bread and coffee. It is a glorious afternoon and I bought some nuts and went out to finish the letter to Erhard. They are having a field day down in Gerardes-sas, the next place to this. We were supposed to go this morning at 3:00 or 4:00 A.M., but due to so many sick boys, they cut it out. The evening was a peach. I retired early tonight. Nothing of importance happened today.

6-8-1918 I got up at 8:00 A.M. I came back, washed and cleaned up. Afterwards I went out in the shade and rested all morning. We need all the rest we can get. I passed the afternoon the same way. Our Company got paid this afternoon. I received eighty-eight francs and sent fifty-seven francs to Norma which amounts to $10.00 for her use. I went out to our place at stand to at night and returned at twelve bells tonight. Nothing more happened of any importance today. It was a glorious warm day.

6-9-1918 I got up at 8 A.M. with breakfast being brought to me in bed. It was a very good breakfast of oatmeal, bread and coffee. After shaving and cleaning up, I went to church services held by Chaplain Danker in the Y.M.C.A. I put my name down in his remembrance book. It was another one of those glorious warm sunshiny days. I said a prayer to Norma my girl over there. I wrote #31 letter to Norma this afternoon out under the trees. During the evening, I was on guard from 4:00 to 8:00 P.M. It rained pretty hard tonight and it got quite cold and windy. I read "The Stars and Stripes" tonight before retiring for the evening.

6-10-1918 I was on guard again from 4:00 to 8:00 A.M. Then I slept all morning. It's a dull gray day. We are making preparations to leave tonight. It is very quiet here today. It seems very dead and lonesome around here. A few of the boys who were away for a long time returned and I gave them the glad hand. An observation balloon is up today. It was rather a noisy night in the barracks. We didn't pull out of here tonight as we expected to. I wrote to Mrs. Aldrich, Dad and Clara Lehmann. Then I retired for the evening.

6-11-1918 Reveille was at 8:00 A.M. There was an inspection of mess kits. It was a dull gray day which cleared up later in the morning. This morning I was on a detail filling sandbags for a dugout for the dressing station. I laid down in the afternoon for a little rest. Then we were ordered to roll our packs, but we didn't move as intended. Mail came in and I received a letter from Norma #45 and one from the Reagans. After I read these, I retired for the evening. I told Mrs. Sheppard of the Salvation Army to write to Norma and she said she would.

6-12-1918 Reveille was at 8:00 A.M. After breakfast mess, I shaved and cleaned up and went out in the shade to look over my letters again. It's another glorious day and rather quiet. I laid around until a detail came around. I policed the barracks after rolling my pack. After finishing my detail, I went over to the Salvation Army hut and bought a piece of pie. What a wild bunch of boys to get it. It was a very pleasant evening and very quiet at the Front. We will not move after all our hard work getting ready. We played a few hands of cards this evening. I attended the midweek meeting at the Salvation Army hut services. I am on guard tonight from 10 to 12:15 P.M. I said a prayer to Norma, dear girl. Wednesday night is my "night with Norma".

[When I read this, my heart really ached for him, because he was missing Norma so very much.]

6-13-1918 Reveille was at 8:00 A.M. It's another glorious day. I washed and cleaned up and had a haircut this morning. There was an inspection of mess kits at 10:00 A.M. I honed up three razors this morning. There was an inspection of canteens at 11:00 A.M. It appeared to me that these inspections were nothing but looking for trouble all morning. In the afternoon I rolled my pack, as we are leaving sometime tonight. I policed around the barracks, etc. There seems to be plenty to do at all times. In the evening there were services at the Y.M.C.A. by Mr. Warron. He gave us a very good sermon, the final especially for the 104th Company, as we are leaving Raulecourt tonight. It's a beautiful evening. We have loaded the combat wagon and are waiting around until the 103rd comes in. They arrived about 12:00 P.M..

6-14-1918 We started on our march at 12:50 A.M. We marched through Sanzey and had four halts during this hike. To brighten the hike and keep awake, we whistled, sang and made merry. A glorious day is before us. We beat the birds this morning. It's pretty dusty on the roads – we look as though we were in a flour barrel. We arrived in Royaumeix at 5:45 A.M. and billeted in the barracks. I have a fair bunk. I slept until 12:00 P.M. and then got up, shaved and cleaned up. In the afternoon I took a stroll through this little town and had a feed of eggs and French fries. It was a very pleasant afternoon. Later I went to Menil-la-Tour. Two letters # 44 from Norma and one from Lucius were awaiting my return. I enjoyed the letter from dear Norma. Tonight I answered this letter to Norma with eight pages #32. I retired after finishing it.

[Royaumeix is in the department of Meurthe-et-Mosell in the region of Lorraine in northeast France.]

6-15-1918 Reveille was at seven bells. It rained somewhat this morning. Andy and myself took a stroll to Menil-la-Tour and had a feed of one dozen eggs a piece. It sure was a filler but we got away with it. After dinner it cleared up fine – was only a bit cloudy. At 2:30 P.M. we had an inspection of rifles and equipment, etc. The inspection lasted about two hours. What a disgusting feeling we had. Now we are going back to the old squads right and left, six hours a day. I guess we are not doing enough. I wrote a letter to Lucius tonight and one to Alice Reagan. I sent an issue of "Stars and Stripes" to Norma. I wrote more letter to friends this evening and was up quite late.

6-16-1918 Sunday. Reveille was at 7:00 A.M. During the time I was shaving and cleaning up, the Boche sent over high velocity shells into this town and hit several of our comrades. It sure was a shaky shave and wash that I experienced. I hurried through and made a bee line for safety. I went to the barracks and put the kit away and decided to leave this place. I no more than left when a terrible whizz bang hit our ball grounds between third base and home plate. The shells were falling so quickly there was no time to duck. At a nearby hotel there were quite a number wounded and killed. There was no dinner mess. We came back, rolled our packs, and made a get away into the fields - something I shall not forget! We came to Menil-la-Tour and billeted here. I went to the entertainment tonight and enjoyed the same. For supper we had flapjacks, bread and coffee. I came back and made my bed and will retire early. It's the Colonel's birthday today. I saw some critical sites today, especially those wounded and killed.

[This was the first time the town of Royaumeix was shelled since the war began and residents were terrified, as related in Clarence Nelson's diary. When it started, they were on their way to church. According to Clarence Nelson's diary, the casualty list included twelve killed and seventeen wounded (four from A Company – Walter and Eugene's Company). This information was provided courtesy of Ellen (Asplund) Racine of the Northborough Historical Society.]

[*Whizz bank* was slang for the noise made by shells from German 77mm field guns. They were fired from high velocity guns and gave you no time to duck.]

6-17-1918 Reveille was at 6:00 A.M. We have a rainy disagreeable day before us. I didn't do much this morning, but I bought some canned goods at the commissary. It continued to rain the rest of the day. During the afternoon, I wrote six letters to Mr. French, C. Krieger, Kate Manning, Stella Chamberlain, Erhard and John Kjellberg. Because it was our turn at the bathhouse, I was ordered to take a bath. After supper mess, I went up to the Y.M.C.A. and got a piece of pie and cup of coffee. After supper, I wrote one more letter to Mrs. French. It cleared up this evening, but is rather chilly.

6-18-1918 Reveille was at 6:15 A.M. At 8:00 A.M, I was detailed at the town incinerator, digging a hole 15x6x5 which was very hard digging through the ledge. It was no fun! We worked in reliefs. It is a beautiful day before us, but cloudy. Many airplanes flew over us today and there were balloons up. I was relieved at 11:00 A.M. for dinner and returned at 1:00 P.M. to the same detail until 4:00 P.M. After returning, I shaved and cleaned up and then we got orders to move. However, it was canceled until further notice. I wrote to Harry Farnum today. Our beloved Chaplain Danker died today for his country as a result of wounds received last Sunday. I retired about 10:30 P.M. The Company went on a working party digging trenches and came back about 1:30 A.M. Battery D 103rd F.A. returned.

6-19-1918 Reveille was at 8:00 A.M. We fell in with mess kits. It rained off and on this morning. Preparations are being made for Chaplain Danker's funeral. The firing squad consisted of A Company Corporal Simmons, Carrigan, Andrews, Roderstrom, Divoll, Wilder, Kirk and Krieger (myself). Sergeant Green was in charge. Three shots were fired and taps were blown. There were many Worcester boys present during the ceremony. Chaplain Danker's brother was present at his funeral. Burial took place at 2:30 P.M. After the funeral, I cleaned my rifle. We had a very good dinner of steak, mashed potatoes, bread and coffee. After supper mess, I went to the concert, but an order came in for a working party at 8:00 P.M. digging trenches. Tonight I started a letter #33 to my Norma but will have to finish it tomorrow. I worked pretty hard this evening. We were taken by truck to the place of work. It rained a little tonight.

[Platoon Sergeant Clarence Nelson reported in his diary that over a thousand men from the division came up in motor trucks. According to Clarence Nelson's diary, the Boche started shelling the town again about 12:00 with a few more casualties and wounded. This information is provided by Ellen (Asplund) Racine from the Northborough Historical Society.]

6-20-1918. I returned from the above detail at 3:00 A.M and was pretty tired, so I slept through breakfast until dinner time. I was with Sergeant McCushion all afternoon and attended another funeral with him. When I came back, I was picked for the same firing squad as yesterday. We were complimented with our good work yesterday. I returned from the burial at 5:30 P.M. This made two funerals I attended today. The detail like last night was called off. I was glad, for I was tired. I retired after writing to Norma, but was too tired to finish this letter.

[I can't imagine how distressing this experience must have been for Walter. Men he knew being blown to pieces—and just nearly escaping himself! It's no wonder he went through periods of depression all the rest of his life with such memories. However, he did try to enjoy life in the midst of this insanity of war. I wish I had found some of his letters to Norma and some of her letters to him. I'm sure their love for each other and his faith in his Heavenly Father helped him through these trying times.]

6-21-1918 Reveille was at 7:15 A.M. I came back from mess, shaved and washed up in time for equipment inspection, etc. at 10:00 A.M. It was a beautiful day and rained just a little which laid down the dust. As I started out for a new gas mask, I was nailed for a detail digging a refuge trench in Royaumeix from 1:00 to 5:00 P.M. After supper mess of cornwilly hash, mashed spuds, bread and coffee, we were told to hang around until 7:30 P.M. in case of need for a working party. It was a nice evening, but there was no place to go. I finished my letter to Norma tonight. I then met Walsh from B Company and had quite a time. I got back to my billet about 12 bells.

6-22-1918 Reveille was at 5:45 this morning. I returned to my billet and policed it. I got ready to go to the rifle range. We left this place on trucks at 8:10 to a place between Toul and Nancey. It was a very nice rifle range to shoot on 200 yards distance. My score was 18 out of 25 out of five shots. The best of the shots were 44 out of ten shots by Corporal Chabot. The best shot of five shots was 24 out of 25 by Corporal Ferrin. After returning and having dinner at 2:00 P.M, I had the afternoon off. I went to Q.M. for a pair of shoes but couldn't get any. It was very windy and blowing hard. I also bought some nuts and finished them. The mail arrived, but none was for me. I made myself scarce after supper. I landed here in the café tonight.

6-23-1918 Reveille was at 7:15 A.M. Sunday. When I finished breakfast, I went up to the washhouse to shave and clean up for the day. It's a beautiful day but windy. I policed the billet for inspection. There wasn't much more to do, so I rested and read a few papers. After dinner, I went up to the Salvation Army and hung around. There were services here this afternoon and the sermon was "Faithful and Loyalty" which was very good. The 101st Band was present and gave us some very good selections which were enjoyed by all. We went to the entertainment tonight. The band concert was very good and the entertainment was enjoyed by all the boys. It was a beautiful moonlight night, but a bit chilly. I retired about 10:30 P.M.

6-24-1918 Reveille was at 6:45 A.M. It's a beautiful day but windy. After I washed and cleaned up, I honed two razors. About 11:00 A.M. I took a walk to Sanzey to B. Battery to see the boys. I had dinner there and came back about time for a short arms inspection at 2:00 P.M. I had a date with the dentist at 3:00 P.M. and had two silver fillings put in. For supper we had a good meal for a change: flapjacks, syrup, bread and coffee. I came to the Salvation Army to get some nuts. The French Division is expected to pull in tonight. We are making preparations to pull out of here soon. It rained a little tonight. I retired quite late.

6-25-1918 Reveille was at 6:15 A.M. I was picked for detail this morning, but I couldn't for my shoes were not fit to wear. I went with Powell scouting up a pair. We finally got a pair, but went through a lot of red tape. These are the best I've had so far. I returned but didn't do anything this morning. We have a beautiful day before us. This afternoon we laid around until about 3:00 P.M. We policed the billets clean, for we pull out tonight. I rolled my pack and made ready to pull out. We had formation at 6:00 P.M. and were pulled down to the field. We stalled around and then went on detail to clean up around the cook shack. We laid around until 9:10 PM and then pulled out. We had one halt on the way to the town of Bruley where we arrived at 11:10 P.M., a two hour hike. We got very good billets. After arrival, I toasted some bread and retired.

6-26-1918 Reveille was at 7:00 A.M. There's another beautiful day before us, with plenty of details cleaning up the town – same old stuff. I washed and shaved and felt better after I dolled up a bit. I took a stroll down to the

Y.M.C.A. but nothing doing here; therefore, I returned to my billet and hung around for dinner. I started out and met Harry Walsh in B Company, took a stroll and went through the church here. It's a beautiful piece of work inside, in back is the chapel which we are told was built in the 11th Century. It's a beautiful piece of work outside also. I put my name on the tower bell. I got nailed for guard duty tonight from 10:30 to 2:30 A.M. I wrote to my Norma after supper # 34 letter eleven pages long. I had quite a chat with Seabry – he stayed with me during the greater part of my guard in the cook shack. It's a quiet night on the coast.

The following photos of the church were taken by Charles W. Robertson and was provided by Ellen (Asplund) Racine of the Northborough Historical Society.

6-27-1918 I was relieved from guard duty about 2:30 A.M. and retired until 10:00 A.M. I was awoken for the purpose of inspection of equipment, etc. We have another beautiful day before us. I washed and cleaned up for the day. Dinner of beef stew, bread and coffee was not very good. During the afternoon, we took a stroll up to Fort Bruley which was some climb up the hill. There's a splendid view from here – a beautiful landscape which I enjoyed very much. Then we went down into the town but before we did, we hit the Groto and the old chapel. I picked up some flowers alongside the chapel and sent them in a letter to my Norma. There wasn't much to do after supper but think of the past and home. We went to the Y.M.C.A. but the same old thing – dead. I came back and retired.

6-28-1918 At 2:00 A.M. I was woken up for guard duty for which I was rather sore, because I was on guard last night too. I was relieved about 6:00 A.M. and didn't eat breakfast except for a piece of bread and jam. We have another beautiful day before us. I slept until about 11:30 A.M. After eating my dinner, I relieved the guard so he could eat his dinner. Then I shaved and cleaned up. I got my pass of six hours for a visit to Toul. It's a beautiful town, but don't think much when a fellow is broke in these cities. In spite of that I managed to see quite a lot here, including a cathedral which took two hundred years to build – a beautiful piece of work. I had three glasses of beer which was some relief. We stayed there until 8:30, then started for Bruley about four kilos distance. We got back about 9:30 P.M. The sunset was beautiful tonight. I retired when I got back after I had a piece of bread and some jam.

6-29-1918 Reveille was at 7:15 A.M. After breakfast, I laid around until the mail came in. I received a letter #47 from my Norma, one from Reagan and one from Norton Company dated June 3, 1918. After dinner, I rolled my pack to move from here. We left Bruley at 2:30 P.M., passed the towns of Pagney, through the outskirts of Toul and arrived in Foug to entrain. It was a hot afternoon hiking on the roads and dusty too. We were very sweaty. I received a "Stars and Stripes" this morning – my picture is in this week's paper. We started from Foug at 8:10 P.M.. and passed through Pagny-Sur-Meuse, Sorcy, Void Sauvoy. It is so dark now that we will have to give it up. We are headed for Paris. It's a beautiful evening and I'm trying to sleep on a flat car, but guess there's no sleep tonight – some shaking up!

6-30-1918 We are speeding along in good style. All I could do was to rest, not sleep. We made a few stops to change the crew and have some mess, but our dear soup gun didn't do much work like the rest of the Companies' did. All I had was hard bread and a cup of coffee on my whole trip – I sure would have appreciated some soup. We passed through some beautiful places. I enjoyed this trip for the scenery, part of it. We saw Paris on the fly and the Eiffel Tower from a distance. We are headed in the direction of Chateau-Thierry. Our trip was about 24 hours on the train. Then our hike started. We stalled in a woods for about two hours, then had the pleasure of having a cup of coffee and hard tack. It was some hike to the soup gun. We started our final hike, and it is stated that we covered about twenty-five kilometers. The boys were extremely tired. The cadence was pretty fast, considering what we had on our backs.

[A soup gun was some type of container with soup in it—probably looked something like a large gun and/or soup probably shot out under pressure.]

[Chateau-Thierry is located in the department of Aisne, in the Province of Champagne in the Hauts-de-France. The battle of Chateau-Thierry on the River Marne is the one that turned the war in favor of the Allies. General Clarence Edwards was in command.]

7-1-1918 We arrived here in this little town of Bois Braudi about 1:30 this morning. I got a fairly good bunk and my bunkie Woodward and I had a can of beans and hard tack before we retired. This tasted good to us. I sure did sleep for it wasn't until 12:30 P.M. that we got up. Our mess was cornwilly hash, French hard tack and coffee. I shaved and cleaned up. I kind of feel the effects of last night. I took a walk around this place which seems a bit cleaner than the places we've already been in. It's a beautiful and warm day. We shared a bottle of wine between us. After supper, we decided to bunk out under the trees where we made a comfortable place which was camplike. Apparently, there have been no soldiers here by the way the people are acting. A French lady cried, because they used her barn to sleep in.

7-2-1918 Reveille was at 7:00 A.M. We had a good breakfast of beans, French bread and coffee. There was another beautiful day for us. We had a drill this morning which I missed – it wasn't intentional. I did a few odd jobs such as sewing, etc. I started out for the Company, but couldn't locate them so I turned back to my tent. It was pretty hot today. We were ordered to roll our packs to move. We're supposed to relieve the Marines. I laid around waiting all afternoon. Something was wrong somewhere. I guess someone got things balled up, for we were told to return to our bunks. We put up a fairly good tent. We had some currants this evening which tasted very good. I retired about 11:30 P.M. It kind of looks like rain tonight.

7-3-1918 Reveille was at 7:00 A.M. At 7:30 A.M. we had mess of roast beef hash, French bread, and oh! such wonderful coffee – no sugar! It wasn't fit to drink without sugar. We fell in for drill at nine bells and returned at eleven bells. We had a talk by the Commanding Officer. I shaved and cleaned up. It's another great day. During the afternoon, we played baseball to fill the bill. After supper, we had an order to roll our packs to move. It came to us suddenly, moving nearer the Front Line with trucks. The 1st Lieutenant gave us a treat today – each one got a cigar and bull. We had a nice ride for the night before the Fourth of July. I had planned to write a letter today, but will try it tomorrow. It was 12:30 when we pulled off the trucks.

7-4-1918 It's a pretty noisy place, like a real Fourth of July celebration. We hiked about seven kilometers to the support lines and relieved the Marines here. We are sleeping in holes about three feet deep for shelter. It's another beautiful day. I slept from 4:00 A.M. to 12:00 P.M. Then I woke up and ate eight ounces of hard tack and cornwilly. We get one meal a day here on the Front Lines. There was the same pounding all day long. I rolled my pack and got ready for a further move. Tonight I lost my outfit on their way into the Front Lines. Someone stole my gas mask tonight and I went back to look for it, causing me to lose my company. I had to walk nine kilometers for another one. I went as far as I dared to look for them. When I came back, I reported to the 2nd Battalion.

[According to Wikipedia, the 104th infantry, indeed the entire 26th Division, was in an area called the Pas Fini Sector (ie. Unfinished Sector). The 52nd infantry relieved the U.S. Marine Brigade in Belleau Wood up to Bussiares. This must be the area where Walter had his gas mask stolen. On July 1, Walter noted that they were stationed at a farm where the woman was crying because they were using her barn. Wikipedia said the troops were in La Loge Farm. As Walter reported in his diary, there weren't any trenches and little wire and a lack of dugouts. They had dug shallow fox holes. Walter reported the same pounding all day long. In Wikipedia, it said that the troops provided supporting fire to the many machine guns. They were near the artillery barrage zone. The American troops were fired on by German artillery and machine guns at all times of the day and night. Walter reported carrying food and water to the troops at the very front line through machine gun fire at night. There were a high number of casualties from mustard gas attacks. Since Walter reported that someone had stolen his gas mask, it was critical that he find another one, which was how he got separated from his regiment in his report above on July 4, 1918. In Walter's account below he mentions dead marines and in other accounts unburied bodies, and body parts in the area. The soldiers must have suffered terribly taking Belleau Wood. Wikipedia referred to it as a forest of horror from the hard fighting earlier in June involving the Marines. The second division and the Marines had stopped the worst of the German advance towards Paris. It was the first battle of Chateau-Thierry.][16]

[Knowing my grandfather, he must have been extremely upset and depressed at the sight of the bodies and the stench.]

7-5-1918 Another day here and plenty of noise and shelling. I started out on a course of instructions to get to the Front Lines, but was lead wrong. I went through an experience of being without anything to eat or drink all day and it was a hot day too. I came to a squad trench and asked them if I was in the Front Lines or near them. There was no answer. Therefore, I went into the trench and shook one of them. Upon so doing, I discovered they were all dead Marines. It was getting dark – this made me a bit scared. I then tore back in the direction from whence I came. I was all sweaty and all in too. I returned to the 2nd Battalion for further details.

7-6-1918 I managed to get some bread and a cup of coffee there, but only a little was spared. Then I lay down for I was very tired. I got up at noon and was sent to report to Regiment H. On my way over there, I was shelled. The Boche must have seen me going through the field. They put one shell through Regiment H before I got there. A runner took me to the 1st Battalion about nine kilometers from here. I got there about dusk so I was kept there until the next day. It was a hot and sweaty day. I had no water all day. There was a continuous shelling and I got very little sleep. I did not get any rest here either.

7-7-1918 With another long day before me, I had only a piece of bread and a cup of coffee this morning. I was told to go in the lines with a runner from here at the 1st Battalion to our Company Platoon Commander. We arrived at the lines in the afternoon about 3:00 P.M. I was all tired out when I got here and was shown my position. Then I laid down for a little rest. We receive only one meal a day in the lines. It was rather peaceful in the Front, but there was high artillery fire to the rear. They shake the daylights when they explode. The woods was ripped to pieces. Night is the most important time when we must be especially watchful. We worked in reliefs of two hours each. We were well covered with machine fire.

[I can only imagine how panicked Walter must have been: losing his gas mask, losing his Company, finding the dead marines, being shelled as he was trying to find his Company, not having any food or water, and not getting any rest. However, he only said he was a "bit scared" at one point when it got dark – he must have kept his cool in order to deal with all of that! I guess that's what soldiers have to do.]

7-8-1918 It's another very warm day. The sun was with us all day. There was plenty of noise, so I got very little sleep. The birds here continue to sing just the same, in spite of all the noise. Night time is here and we are on the alert for what might turn up. It seems to be quiet in our Front Line position tonight.

7-9-1918 It's another beautiful day with the sun out and quiet at times, but very seldom. The rest of the day was passed at rest, but I got very little sleep. A bomb landed quite close to me and the concussion made my head ache. I got very little sleep after this. It's night time and we are on high alert.

[According to Wikipedia, 10,350 shells, as well as mustard gas, were sent over to American lines by the Germans on July 9 through July 14 in the Chateau-Thierry area where the 104th infantry and the entire 26th Division was located. It was reported that fourteen were killed and eighty-four wounded from July 9 through July 14.][17] No wonder Walter had a headache!

7-10-1918 We had another day the same as yesterday and another night, the same as last night – on high alert.

7-11-1918 We were pulled out of the lines and had quite a job getting out, because the Boche kept shelling us so that we had to stay down for some time while exiting. It took some time for all of us, but we got out safely. We were pretty tired and weak from having very little to eat while in the lines. I got as far as the soup gun. Then I had a feed – I ate enough to satisfy myself. We pulled into a woods and I flopped and slept like a log. We pulled out tonight in trucks further in the rear for a parade, because our battalion was representing the 26th Division. We are to be decorated before General Pershing. We went into a woods after we got out of the trucks to finish our night's sleep. We are in La Fere.

7-12-1918 Breakfast was served about eight bells. We laid around until about 2:30 when we marched to a field which was about a five minute walk from here. A rainstorm burst forth upon us so that we were soaked to the skin, but stayed for the ceremony. Decorations were received by the General. Some new heroes were decorated with the D.S.C. (Distinguished Service Cross). Then we returned to the woods again. After this, I went down to a large town about five kilos from here and cashed the check Mr. Kjellberg sent me. I had a very good time on it and came back quite filled. I bought a dozen eggs, cheese, tomatoes, bread, coffee and biscuits. I spent the whole works. About 9:30 P.M. we left in the trucks. We got back to the same place as yesterday and I bunked with Carrigan tonight. It rained throughout the night.

7-13-1918 I got very little sleep. The weather is very wet, raining off and on all day long. We had two meals a day which was very good. I shaved and cleaned up today and felt much better after so doing. Then I laid down and rested, as I feel pretty tired. There's a little noise today on the lines. We changed our positions today – a new location in another woods. It was an all night stand to, since we expected an attack. We were on alert all night.

7-14-1918 It's another warm day, raining off and on. There's nothing much to do but lie around and rest. We need rest anyhow. We were fed twice today and both meals were very good. For breakfast we had flapjacks. For supper we had steak, spuds, bread and coffee. I wrote to my Norma today # 35, answering her letters #46, 47, 48 and 49 all in one. It was the best I could do. I slept pretty well tonight, but it was very wet. It rained pretty hard all through the day and night.

7-15-1918 Another day of rain off and on. We rested around in the woods all day. It is rather a quiet day. We had two meals today. Meals are coming pretty good now. For dinner we had chopped beef, spuds, bread and coffee.

For supper we had a good beef stew, bread, pickle and coffee. There's plenty of noise tonight, pounding away. We were on the alert for a gas attack tonight. About 12:00 P.M. we were ordered to roll our packs. It was a very dark night in the woods, but we managed to get rolled up in due time. We were at stand to all night, expecting something to turn up. It wasn't very cold tonight, so I got what little sleep I could near my pack. The 102nd Regiment got gassed pretty badly tonight.

[According to Wikipedia, the 26th Division was the only thing between the Germans and the open road to Paris. On July 15 there was heavy bombardment from the Boche on the 26th Division as well as mustard gas attacks. Seven thousand rounds of explosives fell on them on July 16 and 17. This is called the Second Battle of the Marne in history books.][18]

7-16-1918 I woke up at day light and unrolled my pack and slept until ten bells. I got up for a breakfast mess of flapjacks, bread and coffee. It was very good. It's a beautiful day and warm. It's very quiet this morning on the coast. I shaved and washed myself today – it was very badly needed. I was on detail today lugging water. I went to the next town and got some chocolate and cigarettes from the American Red Cross. Supper consisted of beef, carrots, radishes, bread and coffee. It's very quiet – not much noise today. There are a few aerial battles overhead. It rained again today and tonight also. I slept fairly well, although I felt a bit restless. I started a letter to Frenchy and Mrs. Thron, and wrote a community letter to Ed Martin with a little bit of news from all the boys from the old 2nd Regiment.

7-17-1918 I woke up with the birds this morning – it looks like another nice day but showery. It was pretty quiet this morning. Once in a while a battery would open up. I send the letter to Ed Martin which had fifty-three names and letters in it. Supper was a good one with steak, beans, bread and coffee. I rested a little and then hiked to the American Red Cross in the next town for some chocolate and tobacco. Also I got a poncho from the salvage heap. We expect to move into support soon, perhaps tomorrow night. It continues to rain – it's now 9:30 P.M. and still light in the woods. It rained pitch forks tonight. At 1:00 P.M. we rolled our packs. We were at stand to - our troops aimed to make an attack to take ground.

7-18-1918 We had a steady hike this morning moving nearer the Front Lines. We expect a counterattack, so are stationed in a neighboring woods. We unrolled our packs here about 7:00 A.M. and then rested, but were ready in case of need. We ate twice today. It's a great day, warm with a little breeze. There was steady firing of artillery all day and it kept moving nearer to us all day long. In the evening we rolled our packs and were issued rations for three days. Then we pulled out in support of the first line. We were at stand to very nearly all night. We are back in our old place that we left on the 4th [I think Belleau Wood]. I rested but couldn't sleep. It's a moonlight night.

7-19-1918 I've been engaged to Norma for one year today. My engagement day is quite different from last year. It's another beautiful day on the coast. We rested all morning and then got up and made our hole a little deeper for safety. There were no eats today, but I scouted up some bread and corn-willy. The American Red Cross sent up cigarettes and chocolate to us boys which was very good of them. There was heavy firing by artillery all day. I have a headache from the noise! Several aerial planes were working today and there were a few battles overhead. Orders came in for all of us to go over the top, so here we're off. Good luck to all!

[According to Wikipedia, the 26th Yankee Division, including the 104th infantry regiment, of which Walter and his brother Eugene were members, were ordered to drive the Germans back from Chateau-Thierry. As related in Walter's diary, the soldiers were on high alert and were on nearly continuous movement in the midst of heavy artillery fire and bombardment as well as being gassed, which was confusing to the troops. [It was reported by the writers of Wikipedia that the men wrote stories involving sacrifice and heroism. That can be seen in Walter's diary account. It turned out to be one of the greatest and most decisive battles in history. The 101st was on the right facing north, the 102nd was in Bouresches facing east, the 103rd was on the left near Lucy de Bocage facing north, and the 104th was in Belleau Wood facing east. The Americans had artillery in the fields to the right and left flanks of the troops. The order to attack came at 4:35 A.M. The Germans dropped severe artillery on the 104th in Belleau Wood. This is where Walter was stationed, before they were ordered over the top, after which he was wounded. The 26th Yankee

Division took part in this second battle of the Marne. The French named them the Saviors of Paris.][19]

The photo below shows guard relief taken by Clarence Nelson in World War I and provided by Ellen (Asplund) Racine, curator of the Northborough Historical Society.

The photo below is a sketch Walter made of the rifle grenades they used during World War I in France.

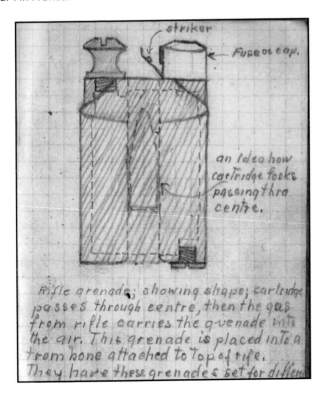

[A local newspaper in my possession published the photos of six Worcester area soldiers who were either wounded or killed in France during battles preceding its publication of August 19, 1918. My grandfather Walter Krieger was one of those soldiers whose photos appeared on the front page. On the last page there was a write-up about his being wounded, as was his brother Eugene Krieger, and that they were both in A Company in the 104th Infantry. However, the account was in error, according to my grandfather's handwritten account. The newspaper reported that Sergeant Eugene Krieger, who was twenty years old, had been seriously injured on July 20, 1918, and that Private Walter Krieger had been slightly injured. According to the newspaper article, the letter to their father Eugene R. Krieger indicated that Walter's injuries were not serious. In reality it was Walter who had been very severely wounded in action in France on July 20, 1918. Walter did not mention anything in his entire diary about Eugene being wounded in spite of some chances he had taken as related in the diary. It stated that their father lived at 24 Brooks Street in Worcester and that they had both been born in New Jersey and educated in Worcester. That was true according to documents I have in my possession. The article reported that Walter, who was twenty-five years old, was recuperating at a base hospital in France, which Walter also related in his diary as well and which follows.]

7-20-1918 Yesterday, I received a bullet wound in my right thigh – it went through my canteen and then got me. I bled like a stuck pig and couldn't go any further in the battle. I was wondering on my way back to first aid if I was going to get hit again, for the air was alive with machine gun bullets! I was also wondering if I'd bleed to death on the way, for I had to crawl about two kilometers back to the first aid station. I was pretty much all in when I got here. (God must have been with me). The Boche also sent over gas which maddened me too. My wound was dressed and I was sent away in an ambulance. The system they had was very good. When I reached another station, my wound was dressed a second time. I was given cocoa and chocolate and then pushed into another ambulance further to the rear. (I learned later in the hospital that Miss Eleanor Kidder Eggleston was born today.)

7-21-1918 After resting here for a few hours, my Lieutenant visited me. I met De Moulpie here for the first time since last winter. He slipped me twenty francs and wished me the best of luck. He told me I would need it, for I was going near Paris. I was evacuated from the first aid station in a truck. It drove slowly to Coulmiers to the #7 station, where I was operated on. The job was successful. When I woke up, a Red Cross nurse was by my bed. I remained here for today. A Y.M.C.A. girl came in and wrote a letter for me to Norma. I was very sick from the ether – a very disagreeable taste.

[Coulmiers is located in the township of Meung-sur-Loire, which is part of the district of Orleans in the department of Loiret of the French region Centre.]

[As Walter's granddaughter, I am very thankful that there were such wonderful surgeons in the Red Cross. He had told me that he had been shot in the leg and had to crawl to the first aid station quite a long way from where he was wounded. However, I did not realize that machine gun bullets were flying over him as he was crawling! He wondered if he was going to get hit again! He never told me that fact. Moreover, it seems to me that he minimized his bravery in all the chaos and terrifying sights that were going on around him during this horrific war. I can now understand why he suffered from periodic bouts of depression. If I had witnessed all of the violence he saw and my fellow soldiers being killed or wounded, I would have had nightmares and depression the rest of my life too. I never heard him complain about anything and it seemed to me he always tried to be positive and look on the bright side of things as he did so often in his diary.]

7-22-1918 I rested pretty well last night, but was very restless. Today I have a few pains, but can not kick because of the sites I see around me with the other patients. I remained here all day. Then I was put on a litter for evacuation, but was not moved until later. I had some very good service here and was treated fine. The day is warm and it's beautiful outside. I feel very tired today, so I will get what sleep I can.

[Unbeknownst to Walter at this time, the Battle of Chateau-Thierry, where he was wounded, was the turning point of the war. Every battalion commander in the 26th Infantry to which Walter was assigned had become casualties.

Although Walter no longer could comment on war events except what he heard from other military personnel, I would like to comment on events which happened to the members of the 104th Regiment in the 52nd Brigade in the 26th Yankee Division where his brother Eugene and friends were still serving. According to Wikipedia, the Americans continued to advance on July 21, encountering stiff resistance from the Germans in the area of Epieds. On July 22 the entire 52nd Brigade attacked Epieds twice, encountering heavy machine gun fire and suffering heavy casualties. On July 23 the 52nd Brigade attacked the Germans again at Epieds, while the 104th Regiment followed a ravine by the side of the road right into the town. The Germans heavily shelled the 104th so they had to withdraw. Again the brave 104th fought fiercely to take Epieds with a group in front drawing German fire while the group in front of the village together with those on both sides attacked so forcefully that the Germans were forced to evacuate the town. This Yankee heroism resulted in an advance of three kilometers. The 26th Division captured seventeen kilometers of previously held enemy territory in a week but suffered 20 percent casualties. In total the 104th took part in six major campaigns, experiencing some of the heaviest fighting with the most casualties of the 26th Yankee Division, including Chemin Des Dames, Apremont, Champagne-Marne, Aisne Marne, St. Mihiel, and Meuse-Argonne. As stated previously, Chateau-Thierry was the turning point of the first world war. Walter's brother Eugene Krieger and Clarence Nelson were among the survivors.][20]

7-23-1918 I was put on a litter this morning for evacuation, but was not removed until 9:30 A.M. There's very good service here by the Red Cross. I was put on a U.S.A. train #53. It sure is some train, which was well arranged throughout. It ran at slow speed all the way, for the comfort of those badly wounded so as not to shake them too much. We had two good meals on the train and the staff was pretty good too.

7-24-1918 I arrived here in Bazou this morning and was quite tired out from being moved around so much. I was quite surprised to land back almost to my starting place: Sartes is not very far from here. This is Base Hospital #116. I am in Ward one, #2 bed. Everything is clean and tidy. I was practically the first one that was brought into the ward. There are Red Cross nurses here.

I spent the afternoon writing to Norma # 36 letter to her. I was glad to be able to write so soon. I answered all her letters up to #49 and #50 from her. Now for some needed sleep.

7-25-1918 I rested fairly well today with a few pains. In the afternoon I wrote a few letters, one to Helen Sawyer, answering her letter, another to my Grandma Martin, and another to Private Leo Lavassu from my own outfit. After finishing, I felt quite tired, so I slept until supper. After supper, I read until I fell asleep.

7-26-1918 I feel pretty well today. I wrote several more letters today to Mrs. Thron, Erhard Kjellberg, Edward Krieger, John Wade, and E.W. Aldrich. It's raining pretty hard today. It's a drowsy day and very lonesome for me. I read the remainder of the afternoon. Then I retired.

7-27-1918 I rested comfortably today. The weather is beautiful and clear today. Eddie's birthday is today – he's 13 years old. I read the papers and a few stories before retiring for the evening. There's nothing more I can say for today's diary.

[Just a reminder: Eddie is Walter's half-brother].

7-28-1918 I am resting quite comfortably today, but at times I am very restless. I wrote #37 letter to Norma today and another to Harriet Hickein to thank her for the Christmas box she sent me which was given to me at the hospital with a number of useful articles in it. After shaving and cleaning up, I wrote a letter to Frenchy. In the evening I wrote to John Kjellberg, Arty Evans, Mrs. Dan Cutler and Mrs. Mary Nye. Then I retired for the night.

7-29-1918 I feel quite well today, only pretty stiff and sore in the leg. I got an alcohol rub this afternoon. It felt fine, because my back is sore from lying down. I wrote to Nils Ebberson today. I read a few papers and then retired for the evening.

7-30-1918 I am resting comfortably today. It's cloudy but otherwise fair. I read all afternoon, for that was all I could do. I had a few visitors here this evening. It was passed very comfortably.

7-31-1918 I slept pretty well last night and am resting comfortably today. After I woke up, I had my daily wash and shave. It's a beautiful day today and warm. Gene sent my diary and booklet over by one of the boys. I was glad to get it again. This afternoon I spent a few hours reading. Sergeant Witt came in for a few minutes to visit this morning. I was fed pretty well today. There was a band concert tonight which sounded good.

8-1-1918 I was awoken at six bells this morning for my wash. After I got cleaned up a bit, I felt fine. It's another beautiful day and very clear. It's very warm and I sweated pretty much. I rested quite comfortably today. Sergeant Witt paid another call. I jollyed with the nurses. I read the papers tonight, then rolled over and went to sleep.

8-2-1918 I slept pretty fair last night, except for a coughing spell. They woke me up this morning to take my wash which sure did feel good. Breakfast was oatmeal, bread and coffee. I shaved and cleaned up after breakfast. The weather is unsettled, raining off and on. We had a good dinner of sliced cornwilly, corn, tomatoes, bread and coffee. I read the papers and then retired for the evening.

8-3-1918 I didn't sleep very well last night, because I had a bad coughing spell. Otherwise, I slept fairly well. I was awoken this morning to take my wash. Temperatures were taken before breakfast was served. We had oatmeal, bread and coffee for breakfast. The French and British retook Soissons today. My wound was dressed this morning – it's healing well. I read a complete novel this afternoon and finished it after supper: <u>For the Money In It</u>, a very good war novel based on the present day. It rained off and on today.

8-4-1918 I slept pretty well last night with the exception of a bad coughing spell. They woke me this morning to take my face wash. It's a beautiful warm day today. I read a little this morning, then shaved and took a bath in bed. Dinner wasn't much today. I took a short nap this morning and when I woke up, Madame Champagne was by my bed. The dear old lady came all the way from Sartes to see me. She brought a cake, an orange and some fresh eggs with her. She walked all the way which was eight kilometers. I was very surprised and, boy, was I tickled to see her again. Many others came from Sartes to visit the boys whom they knew. I wrote letter #38 to Norma, eight pages in all. I read the paper for a little while and then rolled over and said my prayers.

8-5-1918 The nurses woke me this morning to take my temperature and give me my daily wash. After breakfast, the nurse changed the sheets, etc. Then I went back to sleep until about 11 bells. Dinner was served at the regular time – it was a fair dinner. The weather was unsettled today. This afternoon Gene came to see me. We had quite a chat together. I wrote a letter to Gertie Travis in Lowell, Massachusetts and Stella Johnson. I read a little of my book until supper and also the evening papers. The chaplain paid a visit. After his visit, I retired for the evening.

8-6-1918 I had a bad coughing spell last night and again this morning when I woke up. Then temperatures were taken and I washed my face – I felt good after that. For breakfast I had the eggs that Madame Champagne gave me yesterday and coffee. The morning was fair, but then the weather became unsettled. We had a fair dinner for noon mess. During the afternoon, I read a little. I had another bad coughing spell before supper. I don't feel well tonight. It's raining quite hard this evening. Now for some sleep.

8-7-1918 I had a bad coughing spell early this morning. I had my early morning daily wash. It's a beautiful day today. Nothing much happened this morning which I passed comfortably. Noon mess was fair. I spent part of the afternoon sleeping until they woke me up to take my medicine. My temperature was ninety-nine degrees. It was a beautiful afternoon and very quiet. Sergeant Witt and Decent paid me a visit. Then the Chaplain came to see me. He sent in a Red Cross girl with some chocolate and writing paper. I wrote a nice letter #39 to Norma, eight pages long. Then I said my prayers and rolled over to sleep.

8-8-1918 I woke up this morning for my face wash and felt better after it. They took our temperatures. We have another beautiful day ahead of us, but there's little I can do to enjoy it when confined to bed. I dreamed of my girl last night; it was quite a mixed-up dream. Not much of anything happened during the day. This evening I read a little – this seems to be all there is to do. The Salvation Army gave each one of the boys an orange. They sure are doing splendid work. The Chaplain paid me another call tonight before I retired for the night.

8-9-1918 I awoke for my face bath, etc. this morning. We have a beautiful day ahead of us. Nothing very exciting happened today. I feel pretty well today with the exception of an awful headache. This evening was comfortable with a few visitors around my bed telling stories to pass away the time. The chaplain came in to see me just before I got to sleep. I retired early.

8-10-1918 It was rather chilly this morning when I woke up. I had my usual face wash. The nurses took our temperatures before breakfast. Breakfast was served, but it was not at all wonderful. We have a beautiful day before us. This morning they put me in a wheelchair and took me to another ward for local treatment. The trouble with my throat and nose is coming again. I got orders from the doctor not to smoke anymore for a while. Dinner was fair, but scarce. I spent the afternoon reading a good book <u>A Matter of Millions</u> and talking to my next door neighbor. After supper, I read a little. Then I shaved and cleaned up for tomorrow.

8-11-1918 Again I woke up for my face wash. Our temperatures were taken before breakfast. The doctor made the rounds and I was feeling pretty fair this morning. It's going to be a beautiful day today. I slept part of the morning and read the rest of the morning. We had a very nice dinner. We are having such wonderful weather; I wonder what it's doing back home. I started and finished a letter to my girl over there #40 to Norma. Friends from Sartes came to see me this afternoon. I received an invitation to their homes when I get well. They served a fair supper. I read the paper New York Herald. Then I read a little in my book. Now for some sleep.

8-12-1918 I woke this morning for my face wash and to have my temperature taken. I feel better today. It's beautiful out. I read all afternoon and slept some. They sprayed my throat today. I had quite a comfortable evening and read a little. Then I retired.

8-13-1918 I woke up this morning for my face wash and to have my temperature taken. It's a beautiful day today. I'm feeling fair today and they sprayed my throat again this morning. I read a little. Our noon mess was not enough. I read a good part of the afternoon. I sent down for my mail and received #53 from Norma, one from Mrs. Aldrich and one from Norton's. This pleased me so much. I bought two bars of chocolate and some gum with part of the money Norma dear sent me. I retired early tonight.

8-14-1918 Reveille was at 6:00 A.M. I woke up for my face wash and to have my temperature taken. Today marks three weeks in bed. It's another beautiful day. Everybody is all merry and bright. For breakfast we had bacon, rice and milk. I read the letters I received yesterday again. Then I read some more in my book this morning. I was comfortable in the afternoon. I wrote #41 letter to Norma, eight pages long. I wrote six pages to Mrs. Aldrich and another to Norton Company. After writing to Norma, I retired.

8-15-1918 Today is a French National Day. I was awoken at 5:30 A.M. for my wash, but it was a little early for me. After I finished with my wash up, I fell back to sleep. The Chaplain came in and put some water on my forehead which woke me again. Breakfast was not much: prunes and coffee. I spent the afternoon reading and then I slept for a while. It was a beautiful, warm day. Supper was a little better than breakfast and dinner. After supper, Springer came to visit and cut my hair. He brought some nice chocolates with him – a dandy fellow and good barber too. I read until I fell asleep.

[This French National Day commemorates the Feast of the Federation: the Assumption of Mary to Heaven.]

8-16-1918 I woke up at 6:30 for my face wash and fell back asleep until breakfast. It's another beautiful day and pretty warm. The morning was quite comfortable. I had a shave and cleaned up this morning. In the afternoon I read for a while and then had quite a chat with the boys. Lewy Godin came in to see me. It is pretty hot and sweaty today. My voice is very thick today. I passed away the evening reading etc. I dropped a few cards to Norma, Mrs. Hall, and L. Aldrich. There was an airplane doing a few stunts around the hospital. Then I retired for the evening.

8-17-1918 I woke this morning at 5:30 A.M. for my face wash, etc. Last night I had a terrible coughing spell. We have another great day before us. For breakfast we had oatmeal and coffee. This morning was quite comfortable and I read a little. We had a pretty fair dinner. The afternoon was a peach. I wrote a four page letter to Ma Kjellberg [she became his mother-in-law once he married Norma] and sent a poem entitled "Mother" with the letter. I sent "Stars and Stripes" to my Norma also. For supper we had stewed asparagus, bread and coffee. The evening was a peach and I passed it away by reading. A few visitors came to see me. Then I retired for the evening.

8-18-1918 I was awoken this morning by Miss Burkhart. It sure was nice to be awakened like this. I took my daily wash. It's another beautiful morning. Nugent leaves today – he's a good fellow. I was comfortable in the morning - I shaved and cleaned up a bit. After reading the papers, I slept a little. Soderstrom came in for a few minutes. We had a nice dinner today: sliced meat, mashed potatoes, peas, bread and dessert - the best meal I've had since I've been here. It's a glorious day today. I wrote my #42 letter to my girl over there. My friends from Sartes came to see me, and Madame Champagne sent me some plums. I had a dandy supper of potato salad, jam bread, and a piece of cake. I spent the evening reading and then retired.

8-19-1918 I took my wash early this morning. The day is a peach. I read the book <u>Graustark</u> by George Barr McCutcheon today. It was a peach of a book. All of our meals today were very good. I am leaving this hospital tomorrow morning, so I got my things together. I was treated fine here in the Hospital Base #116. The nurses came around to bid me farewell today. They were all very nice to me. I slept very well tonight.

[George Barr McCutcheon was a popular American novelist and playwright who wrote the series of novels that were set in Graustark, a fictional East European country].

8-20-1918 I was awoken this morning by the same nurse. I washed up and had breakfast. Then I was put into a litter to go into the ambulance to the station. I was put into N.C.H. Train. It's another dandy day. There was great scenery all the way. There are nurses on this train. Noon mess was roast beef hash, bread and coffee. I spent the afternoon looking out the windows at the scenery as we passed through Dijon, quite a large town. Since we passed through very slowly, I had a good chance to see everything. I didn't sleep much tonight. I left the hospital here, or rather the station, at 10:00 A.M.

[Dijon is a city in eastern France, the capital of the Cote-d'Or department in the Bourgogne-Franche-Comte region.]

8-21-1918 Today is the fourth week in bed. Our morning breakfast wasn't much, but we had bacon, prunes, bread and coffee. It's a beautiful day for traveling. I enjoyed the trip right through many beautiful places along the way. I didn't lie down until about 12:00 P.M. tonight. Then I tried to sleep, but was constantly thinking of home and my girl.

8-22-1918 I arrived here in Montpont-en-Bresse. I was taken off the train at 2:00 A.M. and put into an ambulance at 3:30 A.M. to be transported to the hospital two and one-half miles from the station. I arrived in bed about 4:00 A.M. I was given a bath and new pajamas to wear. I slept like a log until mess.

I read a little more in my book. Ray Divall came in to see me and I was glad to see him. The hospital is in a Monastery which was built in the 13th century. I wrote a letter to Burkhart and #43 to Norma – only two pages long – I was almost ashamed to send it. I slept very well tonight.

[Montpont-en-Bresse is a small village in the east center of France in the department of Saone-et-Loire of the French region Bourgogne.]

[I think he was almost ashamed to send the letter, because he had been writing much longer letters to Norma. Perhaps he didn't want to write any more, for he didn't want to tell Norma the horror of what he had experienced in that battle. I know my grandmother Norma well - she was a person who worried.]

8-23-1918 I woke up to take my wash this morning until mess was served – it was not like the food we used to get in #116. I wrote three letters today: F.X. Cavannah #116 A.P.O. #731, Gerald Limbach G Company 102 Regiment, and C.O. Company A 104th Infantry for my pay and mail. It's a beautiful but hot day today. Sergeant Clason came in to see me - I was surprised to see him in the hospital. We had quite a chat together. He's down with rheumatism and has changed a lot since I last saw him. I passed the day comfortably. I will now retire.

8-24-1918 It's another beautiful day. Morning mess was corn meal bread and coffee – a bum meal. I do not like this place as well as back in #116. There's not much of anything going on today. I hope I can get up and around; will take a chance at it tomorrow. Service is very poor here, nothing like before. I will retire for the evening before I get thinking too much of home and dear Norma. I must write tomorrow.

8-25-1918 I got up to wash myself, but am very weak today. I had a cane to help myself get around. Breakfast was fair, but … It's a beautiful day today. I managed to get out for a little walk around the grounds – it's a beautiful place. I went down to the river and sat down to write to my girl over there – letter #44. After I finished, I looked at a game of baseball. There were a lot of spectators there, mostly the patients. I fell down twice, but picked myself up and got myself together again. After supper, I went to the movies given by the American Red Cross – they were very good. Following the pictures, I went to bed and slept like a log. They changed me to another ward upstairs here #3-CT#3-E. I had a chat with Sergeant McCutcheon and then retired for the evening.

8-26-1918 It's another beautiful day. I cleaned up and then went for a walk down to the creek. My leg was pretty sore today. It's sunny here and beautiful, but gets very hot in the afternoon. After dinner, I went down by the creek again. I met Sergeant McCutcheon here in this ward – he is at the other end of the ward. We had quite a chat together. I went to the movies again tonight.

8-27-1918 After waking and washing up, I piled over to the mess hall. It's some mess hall – it covers the ground floor of the church. I am feeling better and had plenty to eat. Since it was another beautiful day, I took a walk around the hospital, then visited Sergeant Clason this morning. I met "Soggy". After I had my fill of beans for dinner, I took a walk alongside the creek, visited the laundry, bake shop and the commissary someplace near there. The brook has got some large fish in it, but they don't bite. I came back in time to eat supper. Tonight was a very lonesome one for me. I went to bed feeling very blue.

8-28-1918 Today makes five weeks since I've been in the hospital. I woke up to take my wash and walk to the mess hall. For breakfast we had eggs and coffee. Since I was not feeling well this morning, I went back to bed and slept as much as I could. Dinner wasn't very much but was fair. In the afternoon I was told to stick around until the d octor came. Afterwards, I went out under the trees and wrote #45 letter to Norma. It was only a two-page letter. I played cards with the boys and then went to mess which was about the same as this noon. I came back to my bed and laid down. Sergeant Clason paid me a surprise visit and gave me twenty francs which was very good of him. We went to the movies together tonight. The day was cloudy but warm and beautiful. I slept pretty well. The drive is reported as on.

[I think he meant the American drive against the Germans west of the Meuse.]

8-29-1918 I got up for morning mess which was the same as yesterday. Today is a beautiful day and quite warm. This morning I went out for a short walk and met another fellow named Williams who had been with me on the train. I had quite a chat with him and also saw Bert Forsberg. Dinner was pretty fair this noon. I went for a short walk again around the grounds. It was a glorious afternoon and I enjoyed it out in the woods picking blackberries. I bought two handkerchiefs which I sent to Norma in the next two letters. Supper was cabbage, my favorite. There was an announcement for entertainment which was all French singing and beautiful piano solos. It was enjoyed by all. The evening passed quickly. I will retire for the evening, will close with a prayer and then get some sleep.

8-30-1918 When I got up for morning breakfast, it was rather cold. It turned out warmer towards noon. This morning I went for a walk and came back to help out making beds. I saw Sergeant Green, Sanborn, and Nason. Monk Connors came in the last convoy. In the afternoon I went for another walk around the place. After supper, I went to the movies with Sergeant Clason. I bought some candy today while we were out. We had a pleasant evening and I retired after returning from the movie.

8-31-1918 It was pretty cool this morning. After breakfast, I came back and fixed up the beds. It turned out to be a beautiful day today. I passed most of the morning reading the papers. After noon mess, I went for a walk by the river again and sat down to write two letters – one to Father (#6) and one to Reagan. I gave Dad a piece of my mind in this letter. The afternoon was a peach. After supper I went out in the ball field and laid down for a while. I went to see Sergeant Clason tonight and passed a pleasant evening. Then I went to bed.

9-1-1918 I arose, washed and shaved for the day. I did a few details around to help out. It's another peach of a day. I am in hopes of getting out of here soon. I spent the morning in the ward. Noon dinner was fair. After noon, it rained for the first time since I've been here. I wrote #46 letter to Norma, four pages long, and sent a silk handkerchief with it. The weather was doubtful this afternoon, but it cleared up fine. I saw the ball game. After supper, "Soggy" and myself went up to the Vin house and had a drink. Somebody stabbed another guy in an argument, causing excitement at the hospital. I had a chat with McCutcheon before I went to bed.

[*"Vin house"* is a wine house.]

9-2-1918 Labor Day. I woke up just in time to get to mess. It's a beautiful morning. I came back and made my bed. Then I lined up the beds. I spent the morning in the ward, for the doctor was there to see me and others. For dinner we had beans, dried peaches, bread and coffee (call it coffee?). I went out under the pines, but stayed only a short while. I returned to my bed and went to sleep. I woke up in time for supper. Afterwards, I took a short walk around the place. Today is quite different from last Labor Day when I went to the Fair. I was with Private Claper tonight all evening. Since he was going home, I gave him Norma's address. We had a pleasant evening, but I felt blue and lonesome. I played stud poker, then came back and retired for the evening.

9-3-1918 I got up this morning in time for mess, the same old thing but instead of an egg, we had peaches. It was a very nice day, but very cold in the morning. Later it turned out warm. I went for a short walk. I am feeling very queer lately – nothing that I do seems to go just right. I am very restless and have to keep moving all the time. Noon mess was passable. The afternoon was a peach; therefore, I went for a walk but came back and slept until supper. After supper, I wrote a letter to Mrs. Wade. Then I fooled around and retired after taps.

[Perhaps he was restless and had a need to keep moving all the time, because he had to be constantly on guard when he had been in the trenches. It must have been extremely stressful. In addition, knowing him, he certainly would have been worried about his brother Gene, who was still in action in the trenches. On October 20 he even related a terrible dream he had where he had been captured by the enemy and his brother had been killed.]

9-4-1918 As of today, I have been in the hospital for six weeks. The day is a peach. I went and got breakfast. I came back and made my bed. There was nothing to do but to wait around until the doctor came. Following that, I went for a walk and came back in time for dinner. I returned to the ward. It's getting pretty monotonous here. I went down to the creek and sat around for a while. This afternoon I got a haircut. I wrote a three-page letter to Norma #47 and enclosed the other silk handkerchief. I will now take a nap until supper. Following supper, there wasn't much doing tonight, except to play a few games of cards. We had a lot of fun playing rummy. When taps were blown, we stopped playing and retired for the night.

9-5-1918 I had terrible cramps early this morning, so was awake a good part of the night. I woke up in time for mess. I played rummy with Sergeant McCutcheon and then I was classed A by the doctor. After dinner, I was issued a uniform – I was fitted out pretty well. It felt kind of funny after so long without one. I went for a short walk until supper was served. I wrote letters to Lieutenant Howard and Lieutenant Maynard. I went over and had a chat with Cally Pulver – he's a jolly good fellow. I came back and retired for the night with a prayer for my girl over there. One year ago today the 104th was organized; the 2nd, 6th, and 8th Regiments were combined into two hundred fifty war strength.

9-6-1918 I got up, washed and went to mess, just the same old thing as before. It's a beautiful day ahead of us, but a bit cloudy. I went to see Sergeant Clason today to give him a call. Today I was told that I was to leave in the morning; therefore, I am making preparations to leave, packing up my stuff, what little I have. I'm none too sorry to leave either, as it was getting very monotonous here. I will retire early tonight – up with the chickens tomorrow morning.

9-7-1918 I got up early this morning. After breakfast, I will leave for replacement. I'm feeling pretty well and ready to leave. At 10:00 A.M. this morning I left the hospital bound for the train with others. We were riding 2nd class cars on this trip and had a pretty fair time on the way. They gave me forty-five francs before I left the hospital. This went pretty fast for food, etc. We passed many pretty spots and enjoyed the trip very much. We got off the train at several places and looked the burgs over. A French woman gave me a treat of some wine on the trip. She was very pleasant to talk to – she spoke all Francais. This is all for today – no sleep for me tonight.

[*Francais* is the French language.]

The photo below was taken by C.W. Robertson of Knjizara in the Champagne area of France. Ellen (Asplund) Racine, curator of the Northborough Historical Society provided it to me.

9-8-1918 I was up all morning with no sleep. The train arrived in Tours about 3:30 A.M. The three of us went to look over the town in the wee hours of the morning, hardly anyone was in the streets, and it was some place here! We had a few glasses of wine, etc. to pass the time away. At 6:35 A.M. the train departed, heading for St. Aignan. We arrived here about 9:00 A.M., a very large camp. It rained hard all day! We went through a lot of fall-ins and fall-outs before we were given a classification, clothes, etc. plus a bunk to lay in. Before retiring I wrote three letters - #48 letter to my girlie, one to Pulver and one to McCutcheon. Now I will pound away.

9-9-1918 Reveille was at 5:30 A.M. which is kind of early from what I've been used to at the hospital. We hiked a kilometer or so to mess. I was then sent to get a gas mask which took all morning for instruction, tryout, etc. I got some new dope while at this school. I went through a gas test and then back for noon mess. In the afternoon I went out and shaved and cleaned up. It's some scheme they have here for keeping in touch with a fellow: a punch board and a fifteen minute limit, etc. This sure is a place for discipline. It rained off and on today. During the evening, I went to the Y.M.C.A. to an entertainment that was pretty good. After this I was quite tired out and went to bed.

9-10-1918 Reveille was at 5:30 A.M. It was pouring rain during mess. I was put into E. Company as a company clerk. I handled this job pretty well and am getting along fine. We had a pretty fair meal for dinner. I spent the afternoon pushing the pen. After supper I pushed the pen some more. Tonight I went to a very good band concert. After this, I made out the reports for the day. I retired quite late at about twelve bells.

9-11-1918 Reveille was at 5:30 A.M. After breakfast mess, we evacuated a bunch of men. There was plenty to do until 10:30 when I was sent from here to Spec. Fr. Battalion G.P.O. #927, a camp about twelve kilometers from St. Aignan. It was some place out in the wilderness! It's a nicely arranged camp though. I was put on the records here, and temporarily put in A Prime Class. It rained at all times of the day today. I got a fairly good bunk. One good consolation here is that it has good feeds put into the slate at mess time. I went to the Y.M.C.A. and heard some blacks singing and saw some clever dancing. After a prayer meeting at the Y.M.C.A., I wrote #49 letter to my Norma and then retired for the night.

9-12-1918 Reveille here is at 6:00 A.M. We had a good breakfast mess. It's raining again at all times today. I was put on details all morning at the supply office. Noon mess was good here too. At 2:00 P.M. in the afternoon I was out at exercises and squads left and right until 4:00 P.M. I went and had a shave and cleaned up for the day. Mess at suppertime was good and retreat was at 6:00 P.M. After this, I wrote for my mail at Tours to be forwarded here. I went to the Y.M.C.A. but was turned away, because they were classifying the black troops tonight. I retired early.

9-13-1918 Reveille was at 6:00 A.M. I cleaned up the barracks. Supper was fair. It was a nice day. We had a field exercise in the battery in Tours. Afterwards, I was issued a pass to the Y.M.C.A. and enjoyed myself at the show given by the black company troops. It was followed by dancing and was a pretty lively time. We returned early and I was chosen for detail to unload from the trucks at the supply house. I returned and went to bed.

9-14-1918 Reveille was at 6:00 A.M. It's another nice day. I was sick with a stiff neck, cough and a bad cold. I was detailed to do clerical work classifying the black troops from Camps Taylor and Sherman. It was a very interesting day. Supper was very good. There was retreat at 6:00 P.M. Then I went up to the big event at the Y.M.C.A. I had a good time here at this entertainment. The black boys had a good time too. We had taken thirteen Hun (i.e. German) prisoners in the strike yesterday.

9-15-1918 It's Sunday. Reveille was at 6 bells. I cleaned and shaved for the day. It's a beautiful and quite warm day. I took a walk over to the nearby town today: there are about four houses and a church. I went to church here and saw Chaplain Toques. After dinner, I went to the Y.M.C.A. and wrote #50 letter to Norma. I wrote the commanding officer of A Company for my mail as well as the commanding officer of Base #3. The afternoon was a peach. We had retreat after supper was served. I went to church at the Y.M.C.A. tonight and came back to retire for the night. My bunk fell through tonight, so I had to get into another one.

9-16-1918 Reveille was at 6:00 A.M. We had a good breakfast of bacon, spuds, gravy, syrup, biscuits and coffee. It's a beautiful day. Something exciting happened here for the first time: an airplane landed on our drill field this morning and the crowd was there giving it the once over. I am on a pass for today – the first one I've had since last fall. I cleaned up for the day. I spent the afternoon in the Y.M.C.A. writing and reading. I wrote to my brother Gene and Armory Sawyer who's in Company K, 165th Infantry. After supper we had retreat and then we went to the show at the Y.M.C.A., given by a circuit with the same actors I saw while I was stationed at St. Aignan. I came back and retired for the night.

9-17-1918 It rained very hard after midnight which woke me up. I got up at six bells, almost missed breakfast mess – it was fair. We went out and had a few exercises this morning until recall. After dinner, I went up before the board to try to pass the test to get out of here. However, the commanding officer said nothing doing until I am stronger. All afternoon I laid around and passed up the drill this afternoon. Following supper, I went up to the Y.M.C.A. for a little fun. I came back and retired. It looks like rain tonight.

9-18-1918 Reveille was at six bells. This morning we fell in and had to police and clean up the grounds the black troops left behind. Such a dirty mess! When recall sounded, we returned to the barracks where we hung around until noon. After dinner, I washed up. The weather is fine today with the sun shining. I spent the afternoon out in the fields and woods. I saw a bunch of prisoners that were captured at Chateau-Thierry. They were working with nothing to worry about. I spent the evening writing #51 letter to my girl over there - to my Norma. I went to the Y.M.C.A. for a little while.

[Chateau-Thierry is in the department of the Aisne, in the administrative region of Hauts-de-France, in the historic Province of Champagne. Just a reminder: this was the battle where Walter was wounded].

9-19-1918 Reveille was at six bells. We fell in for exercises and then came back for recall. It rained off and on this morning. We had a pretty fair dinner. We fell in for the afternoon drill. I was picked out for a Military Police company - I was glad to get something like this. There is a company of one hundred in the party for Military Police duty. We fell in for mess at 5:30 P.M. and then they sounded retreat. We moved into tents up on the hill. We went to the Y.M.C.A. and heard a lecture which was very interesting about the past and present conditions of the war. We returned and went to bed. It rained like all fury all night.

9-20-1918 Reveille was at six bells followed by breakfast mess. I cleaned up for the day and policed around the place. It's an unsettled day, very cloudy and muddy. We fell in for drill and were arranged in squads according to height. We had drills all morning with plenty of rests. The weather turned out to be nice and sunny. Noon mess was not very good. During the afternoon, we went out to drill the same as this morning. They issued me the full equipment. We had retreat and then supper. Tonight, I went to the Y.M.C.A. where there was some beautiful music. Three women played violins and the cello. They were great and played several old time songs which were the best I've heard over here yet. My "girl" was with me through and through. I retired for the evening.

9-21-1918 Reveille was at six bells followed by mess. I came back, washed up and got ready for drill with rifles. We worked pretty hard in the field. Following noon mess, we moved to the next town with everything. We thought we were to be on Military Police duty, but we were sadly mistaken, for it turned out to be an escorting company. Somebody has been telling a story. I was on the edge all day. Supper was the best yet: baked beans, pickles, bread, jam and coffee. After retreat I went to the Y.M.C.A. and heard a good sketch. Then I returned to my billet to sleep. I am very much disgusted with life tonight.

9-22-1918 Sunday. Reveille was at 7:00 A.M. The breakfast they served us was the same old stuff: cornwilly, prunes, bread and coffee. I came back to my billet, washed up and got ready for formation at 8:30. We had the rest of the day to ourselves – what a blessing! It's a windy and cold day. We had a very nice dinner this noon and even had seconds. In the afternoon I wrote to Norma #52 letter. It started to rain in sheets and kept up all afternoon. Supper mess was very good also. After supper, I went to the Y.M.C.A. and rewrote the letter to Norma. I met Murray and Gonyea tonight at the "Y". I will now go back to my billet and retire for the evening. I feel pretty tired and lonesome too. Good night, my girlie.

9-23-1918 Reveille was at six bells and drill was at 8:00 A.M. It's a rainy day. At 11 bells we returned from drill and it cleared up a bit. We drilled this afternoon, but it rained so hard that it was postponed. I was issued a helmet and articles, such as toiletry stuff and a safety razor. We had the rest of the day to ourselves. Then retreat was dismissed for the day. Meals were very good today. I went to the Y.M.C.A. tonight, came back and went to bed. I didn't sleep very well tonight.

9-24-1918 Reveille was at six bells followed by mess. First thing this morning they issued me shoes. At eight bells, we fell in for drill. We went through the manual of arms and squared right and left. They gave us setting up exercises and we returned about time for recall. We fell in for noon mess which was pretty good today. The company fell in for gas masks and we hiked to the gas chamber for testing them out. The black troops were there getting their dose too. We returned and were dismissed until retreat. I went to the Y.M.C.A. for a little while. I retired about 9:30 P.M.

9-25-1918 Reveille was at six bells. After policing around the billet, we fell in for the morning drill. We drilled until 11 bells and returned to our little town of Mehers for noon mess. The weather was rather raw in the morning, but it warmed up plenty in the afternoon. We fell in for drill or rather a hike for the afternoon schedule about four kilometers. We returned in time for re-call. They asked who wanted to pick grapes for the French people. The entire company volunteered but nothing has been done as yet. I went to the Y.M.C.A. but nothing of interest was happening so I returned and went to bed. This evening there was a beautiful sunset. I dreamed of home tonight.

9-26-1918 Reveille was at six bells. We fell in for drill at eight bells and it was the same usual stuff that took place. We returned about 11:00 A.M. and had dinner mess. In the afternoon I shaved and at two bells we were brought out for a hike. Instead I was excused for the afternoon, for I was pretty much chaffed (?). It's a beautiful afternoon so I will write #53 letter 6 pages long to my girlie over there, for I didn't write last night. I went to the Y.M.C.A. tonight but came back early and retired.

9-27-1918 Reveille was at 6:00. We fell in for drill at 8 bells, but it was raining and misty, so we hiked past the gas chamber. Then we returned and stopped at the chamber for some boxes for firewood. We came back in time for recall. During the afternoon hike, we returned double timed for about two hundred yards. I returned to my billet and laid down until mess. We had a good supper tonight. After retreat I went to see if my mail had been forwarded, but none as usual. I went to the Y.M.C.A. and returned about 9:30 when I retired for the night.

9-28-1918 Reveille was at 6:00 A.M. We fell in for drill and marched over to the drill field, but only stacked arms. We then marched over to the office to give our names to the new company roster known now as the E Company Escorts. We returned for recall and had a very good dinner. This afternoon we had inspection of equipment and rifles. I passed OK. The rest of the afternoon we hung around until retreat. Several airplanes were flying overhead this afternoon. It was a misty day. I shaved and cleaned up for the day. We had retreat at 6:00 P.M. I went to the Y.M.C.A. and returned about 9:30 P.M. for bed. I got a good bunk mate Thomas Blackburn.

9-29-1918 The Bulgarian Armistice was signed today. Reveille was at 6:00 A.M. Breakfast at 6:30 was a bum one at that! We rolled our packs and made ready to leave this place at 8:30. We laid around until it was our turn to pull out. While we were waiting, the Y.M.C.A. gave each one a box of matches and cigarettes. We left here at 9:30 for St. Aignan and are now known as the 58th Company Escorts. We pulled out in trucks and boarded the train, the same as usual box cars. We left the train station about 12:00 with three days rations each. During the afternoon I enjoyed the scenery part of the trip. Supper was served on the fly. There was no sleep on the train tonight. We passed a place tonight called Le Mans where we were supposed to get coffee, but nothing doing. I was on guard tonight. It has been one year today since I've seen Norma.

[Bulgaria entered the war on the side of the Central Powers on October 14, 1915, when it declared war on Serbia. It had lost ninety thousand soldiers during the course of the war.]

9-30-1918 We are still traveling on the route toward Paris. We circled all around Paris today. It was pretty chilly all day. Breakfast was a light one. The scenery was very pretty on the way. We saw a load of prisoners this afternoon. It rained pretty hard this afternoon at about 2:00. We had some vin rouge. I saw the Eiffel Tower from the same place I saw it last time. We made several stops on the way. It's a tiresome rubbly way to travel. It rained a little this evening – not much sleep.

[*Vin rouge* means red wine.]

[Walter certainly seems more at ease with himself now that he is back with troops. However, I think he misses his friends and, especially, his brother Gene in Company A. I know he is missing Norma and his family back in the States, as he mentions that it has been one year since he has seen them. As I read all of this, I can feel his loneliness. Family and friends were always extremely important to my grandfather.]

10-1-1918 We're still on the road, getting nearer our destination. The weather is rather cold. There's nothing more to report right now – only a lot of scenery I've never seen before. Evening was passed away, trying to sleep a little. We passed through Saint-Dizier this evening about 6:00 P.M. There was a car full of bread alongside of the train. Since the boys didn't have any eats left, they had the nerve to steal what they could. The people at the station got tipped off about it and put a guard on.

[St. Dizier is in the Haute-Marne department and the Champagne-Ardenne region 192 kilometers from Paris—part of the Grand-Est region].

The photo below was taken by C.W. Robertson and provided by Ellen (Asplund) Racine of the Northborough Historical Society.

10-2-1918 We are still going but very near the place to disembark. We're getting nearer the Verdun Front. We arrived at our destination at 8:00, unloaded and pulled into a town named Souilly, with a large prison camp. We pitched tents and are now resting until night, for we go on guard tonight. I went down to the creek to wash and shave, so I feel much better now. We can hear heavy firing on the Front – it's very plain from here. I have a good bunkie now and we both sleep together in a pup tent. I didn't sleep very well as it was very cold on the ground. My mail address is P.W.E. 58th Company Enclosure #3 American Expeditionary Forces, France.

[Souilly is a commune in the Meuse department of the French region Lorraine in the district of Verdun in northeast of France. The Town Hall served as headquarters for General Pershing during the Meuse-Argonne Offensive in 1918.]

10-3-1918 Nothing of importance occurred today, it was the same routine as yesterday. The weather is very raw this morning. This evening I was put on guard at the Pen. Acting Super – not hard. I have two hours on and four hours off. I slept better tonight, because we had more blankets and straw to sleep on.

10-4-1918 One year ago today we started on our trip to France. After breakfast, we were told to move from our pup tents to the barracks inside the prison gates. I got a fairly good bunk. We are acting as Headquarters Company Prison Escorts until further notice. My detail is to see that all men we get are checked in and those we get rid of are checked out. Not so bad. The weather is not so bad, but it's still rather raw and damp. There's always something doing. During the evening, I was relieved to get rested up. I slept fine tonight, as we had plenty of covers over us.

10-5-1918 There was no reveille this morning, but I got up for a very good breakfast. I was on duty right after I finished my meal. It was a very misty morning, but the sun came up and cleared the mist away. There's nothing rushing to do this morning. The afternoon was nice. For the evening I stayed here at the check room until 5:30 P.M. and then went to bed.

10-6-1918 I got up for breakfast and then went on duty. It was very misty again this morning, but cleared up about noon. A number of prisoners came in this afternoon. It's a rushing business. I went for a short walk to the Y.M.C.A. and got some paper so I could write to Norma my #54 letter to her.

I also wrote to Reagan, Erhard, Clason, and J. Aldrich. Also I wrote a letter to request my mail. I went to the Y.M.C.A. but nothing doing there so I came back to the check room.

10-7-1918 I got up, had breakfast and reported for duty. It's a muddy, disagreeable day today, misty all day long. I had only three entries today. There was nothing to do but lay around. We are eating very well here, much better than I ever ate since I've been in the service over here. We had a little hail storm. I retired about 8:30 P.M. I was pretty sick tonight with the runs.

10-8-1918 I got up several times with the runs – there's no fun in it! I was awoken twice to check up the new prisoners coming in. It's a sloppy day and very muddy. I was taken off the check job and changed around. I didn't do very much. I spent the afternoon fixing around my bunk. The evening came and I was put on detail issuing blankets to the prisoners. I finished this detail about 12:00 P.M. I came back and retired.

10-9-1918 I got up for breakfast and was on detail carrying water to the kitchen. It's a nice day today. I policed around the bunks and made beds, etc. The afternoon was nice. I was on detail all afternoon. I spent the evening reading and then went to bed.

10-10-1918 Reveille was at 5:45 A.M. I worked in the supply house all morning. After noon mess, I worked in the supply house again. I worked with some of the prisoners this afternoon. I returned in time for supper and was pretty tired and retired for the night.

10-11-1918 Reveille was at 5:45 A.M. I worked on the gate today checking the prisoners coming in. I finished this and had the rest of the morning to myself. It's a nice day today. For the afternoon I was on detail. For the evening I went to the Y.M.C.A. and bought some candy, the first I've had since I left the hospital. I retired for the evening.

10-12-1918 Reveille was at 5:45 A.M. I policed up the barracks, washed and shaved. We had inspection this morning. It's a pretty good day. In the afternoon I was on duty checking in the prisoners. There are lots of them here now. It was raining all day and very muddy. We are getting rumors about peace terms now. Everybody is enthusiastic about it this evening. Secretary Baker's here in this town. I retired for the day.

[Newton Diehl Baker was President Woodrow Wilson's Secretary of War from 1916 to 1921.]

10-13-1918 Sunday. Reveille was at 5:45 A.M. I was giving an inspection of rifles this morning. It's a rainy dismal day and talk about muddy – whew! I can't pity the Boche much – they sure are a soaking mess! Dinner was a peach: beef pie, mashed spuds, apple pie, bread and coffee. During the afternoon, I went down to the Y.M.C.A. and started a letter to my girl over there, #55 letter to Norma. I didn't do very much today, but cleaned up a bit for the day. I had two cups of cocoa at the Y.M.C.A. which was pretty good. The Captain gave a talk this afternoon discussing several things for the good of the outfit, since I can't get back to my own outfit anymore.

[Just a reminder – the Boche are the Germans.]

10-14-1918 I got up for breakfast and then made my bed, etc. It's a rainy day and very muddy – such weather - raw and dismal! There was not much for me to do this morning. After dinner, I made a new foundation for the kitchen stove with mud and bricks. I finished it after supper. I felt pretty tired after I finished the job, but it was very satisfactory to the cooks. There won't be so much smoke anymore. I retired for the evening.

10-15-1918 After breakfast I policed the barracks. The daily routine was the same as yesterday. I went into the kitchen to see the stove, etc. I came back and laid down. It was the same old weather as yesterday – rainy and muddy. I am getting a bad cough, but am glad we are in the barracks and not in those pup tents. I was on detail this afternoon with the prisoners. I retired quite late tonight. It's raining hard just now.

10-16-1918 After breakfast, I came back, made the bed and cleaned up. It's another rainy, disagreeable day, dismal and lonesome to me. And still the war prolongs with no change. I went and had my hair cut and a shave, costing me the sum of thirty cents when pay day arrives, but <u>when</u> will that be? During the evening after supper, I went over to see Sergeant Searles from C Company 104th. He is here with us. I had quite a chat with him. He gave me twenty francs, as he knew I was broke. I played cards tonight, thinking I would be lucky, but not tonight. The rest of the evening my thoughts were with those at home.

10-17-1918 I got up for breakfast of beans, milk and coffee. I had two meals this morning. Then I reported on a new job at G. 2 for duty there as a runner. It's a very bad rainy, muddy day. I was issued heavy underwear today. I had a very good dinner this noon. This afternoon I was on detail where I read a little and played a few games of solitaire by myself. This evening I went over to the town and had two bottles of beer. I retired quite late tonight. I was in Halifax at this time last year. It's a birthday - whose? Grandma Martin?

10-18-1918 I got up for breakfast and then reported to G.2 for duty. The day turned out to be a peach with the sun shining, although it was very muddy. I worked all morning and afternoon in relays. The duty is not very hard. I am seeing some interesting things in this line of duty. During the evening, I went to the town and had a few glasses of beer (near beer?). When I returned, I went to visit Sergeant Searles and a few cigars were passed around. Afterwards I fell into a card game so was up quite late.

10-19-1918 After breakfast I reported for duty with the same routine at G.2 as yesterday. The weather was fair today although very cloudy. Today I did various details. This afternoon was quiet so I read a little and then played cards. This sure is a different life from what I used to have before I was wounded. Although it is very monotonous, it is still very interesting. During the afternoon, the weather turned misty. All of the meals were very good today. Evenings here are very lonesome. I have a longing feeling for news from home. I'm not getting any of my mail. Tonight I sewed on two service chevrons. I will retire early, for I was late getting to bed last night. Tomorrow I will write to my girlie "over there."

10-20-1918 After breakfast I reported for duty at G.2. It's a miserable day raining and very sloppy. There wasn't much to do this morning so I started a letter #56 to Norma which I will finish this afternoon. The afternoon was the same as the morning. I read a few short stories. After supper, I was on duty until eleven bells. During this time, I wrote another letter #57 to Norma and sent a poem with it entitled "Little Pal o' Mine" (below.) Two letters to her in one day isn't bad. I went to bed about 11:30 P.M. tonight. I dreamed that I had been captured and Gene had been killed. I was freed again by a reinforcement. It sure was some dream! This engagement took place back in the states.

Just a wee remembrance Of a little child so fair,

From Dad, who coaxed himself away To leave you over there.
Just a little thought or two, A dream, a wish, a prayer,
For you, my little smiles girl, Across the sea back there.
Just a bit of Daddy love, To you I send it all,
Your eyes, your smile, your golden hair, Your love for "raggy doll."
Just a little tear sometimes – Yes, men they weaken too.
War is hard, but harder still Is being away from you.
But just as sure as can be When summer comes, you'll find me
Me back in Worcester With you, Lil' Pal of Mine.

[These are not the words attributed to David Carb of the American Red Cross in "Little Pal o' Mine" compiled by Herbert Adams Gibbons in SONGS FROM THE TRENCHES . I don't know where Walter found these words. Perhaps he made them up himself.][21]

10-21-1918 Following breakfast, I reported to duty at G.2. This morning I made the fire and cleaned the office. The weather is better today with the sun shining a bit. Dinner was very good. I spent the afternoon with the same routine as this morning. It's rather quiet here in the office with practically nothing for me to do, so I played a few cards between times. Supper was very good, but I wasn't very hungry. I came back to the office and laid around. After duty I went to see Sergeant Searles. He had a dandy collection of German post cards and photos he got from the prisoners. I then went to the Y.M.C.A. but came back right away to the office and had a sandwich before leaving for bed. It's a bright moonlight night.

10-22-1918 After breakfast, I reported for duty at G.2 where I made the fire and cleaned the office. It's another great sunny day. I worked all morning doing various things in the line of duty. Dinner was very good. The afternoon was quiet with only a few odd things to do. I shaved and cleaned up a bit. I read a little and then played rummy with the boys. Supper was very good with doughnuts for dessert. After returning to the office, I wrote a letter to P.L. Cosman. I left the office about 10:30 P.M. and went to bed. I feel a bit tired tonight. After I wrote a letter to my girl, I wrote the words to "What a Friend We Have in Jesus" which I enclosed in her letter. The day following my writing of the lyrics, the composer Charles Converse died at the age of eighty-five years. Strange, wasn't it?

[Joseph M. Scriven, a preacher, wrote the lyrics that depict a deep understanding of God and Jesus, which are particularly helpful during times of loss and loneliness. His fiancée accidentally drowned the night before they were supposed to be married. Walter's fiancée Norma was an excellent pianist who could play this song.]

10-23-1918 After reveille and mess, I reported to duty at G.2, made the fire and helped clean up the office a bit. Today is a very nice day. I did various things about the office this morning. Dinner was very good. The afternoon was the same – quiet. About 3:00 P.M. I went to the Red Cross to get some reading matter and writing paper. I got several books and magazines to read. On the way I met Jack Cain, strolling along. He was quite surprised to see me. We had a long chat together. I got several books and magazines to read. I got back about 4:30 P.M. After supper, I came back to the office and witnessed a Court meeting of a Lieutenant charged with several things. It turned out to be only a joke on him. Although this was only for learning, it all sounded real and was very interesting to hear. I retired for the night.

10-24-1918 Reveille was at 6:00 A.M. I reported for duty at G.2. After making the fire and cleaning up the office, I worked all morning. During my spare time, I played rummy. We had a beautiful day. After dinner, there was not much doing, so I laid around for a while. This evening in the office, I fed six Huns. Then there was nothing else to do, so I read a few short stories. It was a very long evening for me. The first part of the night was very dark, but then the moon came out. I went to bed about 11:00 P.M.

[Just a reminder, Huns is another name for the Germans.]

10-25-1918 Reveille was at 6:00 A.M. I went to breakfast, made my bed and then reported to G.2 for duty. After starting the fire and cleaning up the office, I was a bit hungry so had some tomatoes with bread. We played a few hands of rummy. The rest of the morning we were at work. Dinner was very good today, but I had a severe headache. I laid down and felt somewhat relieved. After supper, I went back to the office. I remained until I could not stand the headache any longer. I went to the infirmary and got some aspirin tablets. Then I retired.

10-26-1918 Reveille was at 6:00 A.M. I had the same duty as yesterday. The weather was a peach. I cleaned up the office a bit. It was quiet today. I retired about eleven bells.

10-27-1918 Reveille was at 6:00 A.M. It's a very nice day today – a Sunday. I reported to G2 for duty today. I made a fire and cleaned up the office and worked all morning. They took our blankets and gave us three new ones as well as a new bed tick. This afternoon I worked a little, cleaned up and shaved, etc. I got a new O.D. shirt this afternoon. During the evening, I wrote a letter to my girlie over there #58. Mail was postponed until Wednesday. It was quite late when I finished duty and went to bed.

10-28-1918 Reveille was at 6:00 A.M. I reported to duty at G.2 for our daily routine. I made the fire and cleaned up the place. The duties were the same as usual. During the afternoon, there wasn't much to do. I played Casino with the boys here, so time went by fast. Then I received a letter from my brother Gene with twenty-five francs in it. This was the first mail I've had since I was in the hospital. The day was a peach. I was broke until luck came my way, thanks to Gene. I wrote a letter to Gene tonight.

10-29-1918 Reveille was at 6:00 A.M. I reported to G.2 for duty. It's a very nice day. I spent the evening with Sergeant Searles.

10-30-1918 Turkey's Armistice was signed today. Reveille was at 6:00 A.M. I reported for duty at G.2. It's a very nice day. There was a big fire this noon, burning several buildings and destroying the telephone exchange. It cut off all communications. It was an exciting time. I was on the pumping detail pinned in between two buildings. They poured water on us so we wouldn't get scorched. We worked like h____all through the afternoon until the fire was out. Afterwards we went to dinner. I was like a drenched duck. I wrote letter #59 to Norma today. Then I retired quite late.

[Turkey's Armistice was signed at the port of Mudros on the Aegean island of Lemnos. This ended the Middle Eastern hostilities between the Ottoman Empire and the Allies. The Russians also withdrew from the war.]

10-31-1918 Reveille was at 6:00 A.M. There was no breakfast for me as I wasn't very hungry. I ate later in the morning. It is a peach of a day. I worked all morning in G.2. The afternoon routine was the same as this morning. I shaved and cleaned up. During the evening, I was on duty until 10:30 P.M. Then I retired.

11-1-1918 Reveille was at 6:00 A.M. I reported for duty at G.2 where I made a fire and cleaned up for the day. I worked all morning. Noon mess was fair. During the afternoon I cleaned up a bit. I worked all afternoon as a runner. It was a nice afternoon. Evening was rather quiet. I stayed in the office until 10:00 P.M. and then retired.

11-2-1918 I got up for breakfast and reported for duty at G.2. I didn't get here early enough to make the fire. We had a busy morning with an inspection. It's a beautiful day. We had a very busy time this afternoon handling many prisoners. During the evening, I worked quite late on a searching party for prisoners, that is going through officers' pockets for things they are forbidden to have. It rained and was very disagreeable tonight. I retired around 11:30 P.M. and was very tired. We had good news about an Austrian Armistice.

[The Austrian Armistice was to be signed at Villa Giusti near Serravalle, Italy.]

11-3-1918 Sunday today. Austria signed the Armistice today at 3:00 P.M. This sounds pretty good to me so far. I got up for breakfast which was dough-nuts – it was great. I reported for duty at G.2. I was on time to make the fire. We have another busy day before us, for there are many prisoners coming in. I was issued a leather coat and boots this morning. Noon dinner was very good. During the afternoon, I was pretty busy around the cage. It was pretty muddy outside today. Many prisoners are now here and more are coming later. I feel very tired tonight and will not be able to write to Norma. I will try to get one written Monday or Tuesday. I will now retire.

11-4-1918 Breakfast was at 6:00 A.M. and I reported for duty at G.2 where I made the fire and cleaned up the office. It's still sloppy outside. I worked all morning running to G.2 and back. The weather is fair with the sun out. Following dinner, I worked all afternoon. I stayed here in G.2 all evening until quite late. Then I retired. Austria is now finished.

11-5-1918 Reveille was at 6:00 A.M. as usual. After making my bed, I reported to G.2 for duty. I made the fire and cleaned up for the day. I worked all morning in G.2. We have a very nice day before us. Dinner was good. During the afternoon, I read a little during my spare time. Now is the interesting part of the war: good news is coming in every now and then. I was on duty in G.2 all evening until quite late. Then I retired for the night.

11-6-1918 Reveille was at 6:00 A.M . I reported to G.2 and made the fire, then cleaned up the place for my morning exercise. It was a fair day and warm.

I worked all morning – it was very busy this morning. The afternoon routine was the same as the morning. During the evening, there was good news from a party of delegates from Berlin enroute to Paris to discuss Peace terms. They came through at Haudroy. Berlin was bombarded from the reports. I was in the infirmary when this happened: I was there getting fixed up? I wrote to Norma #59 letter, Frenchy, Charles Krieger, Aldrich and Hall. I retired at 12:30 A.M.

11-7-1918 Reveille was at 6:00 A.M. I reported to G.2 without eating breakfast this morning. I made the fire and cleaned up for the morning. Splendid news came in with good results everywhere. This afternoon it rained pretty hard. I worked on the same routine as this morning. This evening I took a bath and laid around in the office reading between times of fatigue. I retired about 10:15 tonight.

11-8-1918 Reveille was at 6:00 A.M. I reported for duty at G.2 making the fire and cleaning up the place for morning exercise. Then I started my daily routine. Better news comes in every day. It's a rather foggy day, but still muddy outside. Dinner was tomato soup, bread pudding and coffee. The afternoon was the same as this morning. I met Jack Miller from my old outfit this afternoon. He was looking fine, dog robbing for a Lieutenant in 96 Company Escorts. I spent the evening in the office reading, but on duty in case of need. I retired for the night.

11-9-1918 Reveille was at 6:00 A.M. It's a glorious day today. I made the fire and cleaned up. Then I reported for duty at G.2. I worked all morning at the office. Noon dinner was very good. In the afternoon I continued my former duty. It was a pleasant afternoon but still very muddy. When the evening came, I went over to see Sergeant Searles. He received several papers from Worcester, amongst them was a picture of my girl. Wasn't I feeling lonesome when I saw that picture! I have something to write about now. Also I got twenty francs to buy some presents for my girls and friends for Christmas. Now for some sleep.

11-10-1918 Reveille was at 7:00 A.M, being Sunday, an hour later. I reported to G.2 for duty, made the fire and cleaned up for the day. We have a beautiful day before us. There's nothing to do this morning so I took things easy. I spent the afternoon the same as this morning. This evening good news came for all of us: Germany will sign an Armistice this evening. I wrote a letter to my girl #60 and sent several post cards: Norma, ma, pa, My Pop, Gramps,

Aldrich, French A. It's a wild evening around here – everybody is celebrating, drinking, etc. But I felt too lonesome to enjoy it. I passed the evening with good thoughts of my girlie over there. Now for some sleep.

11-11-1918 Hostilities ceased at the eleventh hour on 11-11-1918. Following reveille at 6:00 A.M., I reported to G.2 for duty. Things have let up since the armistice was signed. Everybody here has big heads this morning. This afternoon I took things easy as there was nothing of importance to do. This evening thirty-seven Russians came in and some prisoners also. Afterwards, I went to see Sergeant Searles and passed a few minutes with him. He showed me several things in the souvenirs he's got. Some collection! After I returned, I had something to eat and went to bed. My Bunkie had a bunch of money stolen from him this afternoon. Some kind of trick it was! I felt bad although it wasn't stolen from me.

[The German Armistice was signed at LeFrancport in Foch's railway carriage near Compiegne in the Oise Department in the Hauts-de-France, ending the fighting on land, sea, and in the air. It was a complete victory for the Allies and a complete defeat for Germany.]

11-12-1918 Reveille was at 6:00 A.M . I reported at G.2 for duty, but arrived a little late this morning. The fire was already made and things were going along fine, making it quite easy for me. It's a nice day today. I went to Souilly today and got some nuts. I saw John Miller again. He leaves here today. Bells were ringing their merry tones today and people were cheering. There was a band concert this morning in town. The bells were too much for the band, so they cut the music short. During the evening, we had a good time amongst the boys here in G.2 singing and telling stories. Then we retired for the day.

11-13-1918 I got up but didn't eat breakfast at the kitchen this morning. I reported to G.2 for duty. It's a cold day although the sun is shining. Things are letting up here in G.2, meaning they will soon relieve us here at this line of duty. I came back to the office, but being my last day here, I will take things easy. I packed up what I had here. I was relieved here tonight. We were complimented by the Sergeant in charge for the good work we did here. I will retire early tonight, for we will have reveille for the first time with a roll call.

11-14-1918 Reveille was at 6:15 this morning, followed by roll call. It was pretty cold getting up this morning. I was detailed to another job, this time in the infirmary, taking sick prisoners to the hospital, etc. Again this is another interesting line of duty. Things went along very nicely this morning. It was a beautiful day, but very brisk. I made one trip to the hospital with two Boche at noon time. The afternoon slid along very fast. At suppertime I had another trip to the hospital with one Boche who was a very sick dog. The 26th Division is pulling through this part or sector. I saw some of them. I will now try to get some sleep.

[Remember that the 26th Yankee Division was Walter's original division before he was wounded on July 20, 1918 and still was Gene's as far as I know.]

11-15-1918 Reveille was at 6:15 A.M. It was pretty cold this morning. After breakfast, I dressed up for duty at the infirmary. I have a very pleasant job here. This morning I made a trip to the hospital with three Boche. I saw some of my old Division this morning passing through this place. It made me feel sad that I couldn't go along with them. Rumors state that they are homeward bound! It's brisk out this morning, but the sun is shining. During the afternoon, I made another trip to the hospital with seven more Boche. I spent the rest of the afternoon in the infirmary. Several letters reached me today. I answered some but not all of them: Chamberlain, French, Harold Gilmore, Travis Evans, Manning, and Charles Krieger. Today I also received a card announcing the birth of a child born to Mr. & Mrs. Eggleston on July 20. Now I will go to bed for it's almost 10:30 P.M.

11-16-1918 Reveille was at the usual hour. Then I made my bed for today is inspection. I reported for duty at 7:30 and took things easy until the tide came in. I made a trip to the hospital with three Boche. While here at the hospital, I went to the Red Cross and got some candy, towels, soap, a toothbrush, magazines, cigarettes, etc. I came back and read the magazines. While reading, I was handed a letter from my girlie over there #52. I felt so bad and lonesome that I was good for almost nothing at all. This was some letter and a touchy one! The evening passed very pleasantly. The Boche prisoner that's here working in the infirmary is a pretty good fellow. He's married and has a little girl back in his home. He didn't like the war at all, like many of the other prisoners here told me. Being of German heritage, Walter spoke German although he and his parents had been born in the U.S. It's about 11:00 P.M. now.

11-17-1918 Sunday. Since there was no reveille this morning, I slept later. When I got up, I reported for duty about 8:00 A.M . It's a very nice day today.

I was quite busy this morning. I made a trip to the hospital with two Romanian and two Italians. One Romanian was unable to help himself, so I helped him in the receiving room at the hospital. He was so happy he cried and kissed both of my hands for the little help I provided him. This shows how badly he must have been treated in Germany's prison camp. An example of the Germans! For the afternoon I was on duty here and then made another trip to the hospital. When evening came, I started a letter #61 eight pages long to my girlie over there. I am not feeling well tonight. I went to bed quite late about 11:00 P.M.

11-18-1918 I got up for breakfast and then reported for duty at the infirmary at 8:00 this morning. It's a very pleasant day. The Captain and Lieutenant doctors leave us today. New ones are taking their places. There was pretty much to do this morning. I made trips to the hospital with three Boche this morning. The afternoon was a little easier for me, since I made only one trip with one Boche. The American E.F. Third Army consisting of 1st, 2nd, 3rd, 4th, 5th, 26th, 32nd, 42nd, 89th and 90th Divisions of about 250,000 men with Major General Dickman in command are making their advance towards the German border. I'm still on duty in the office. I intended to retire early tonight. However, I went over and helped out the officers with serving at a good time here. Several officers and Hello girls were having a good time dancing, playing cards, etc. Nothing made me feel so near home as tonight. I didn't get to bed until after 12:00 P.M.

11-19-1918 Reveille was this morning but instead of eating, I laid down until 8:00. Then I went to the office. I had some of the goodies we had left over from last night. I feel quite tired today from being up so late last night. Things went along nicely here in the office. I am on another duty in the office now, pushing the pen. Things are coming along pretty nicely now. I am here interpreting for the officers also. The day was warm and pleasant. Thoughts for home going now are on my mind. In the afternoon there wasn't so much to do. My barber is a little Boche man who also shaved me and my orderly is a Boche man who does my washing and dishwashing, making it a little easier for me. This evening I was at work in the office. Tonight a letter "A" was put on my left arm representing 1 Army Headquarters. Now for bed.

[Just a reminder: being of German heritage, Walter spoke German.]

11-20-1918 Reveille was this morning and then mess was served. I came to my office and took up the daily work. I was quite busy this morning writing - I had quite a bit of paperwork to do. It's a very nice day today. I ate dinner at the usual time. I worked all afternoon. A Hun man who was sick kind of put me out. I sent a few to the hospital today with influenza in both cases. During the evening, I had a few visitors. My bunkie came over and we had coffee. Then he wrote a few letters while I was busy with paper work. I was issued a new uniform today. Our artist drew my picture, but did a bum job on it. He will try again. I will retire early tonight as it's now quite late 10:00 P.M.

11-21-1918 This day was precisely the same as yesterday. It was a busy day for me. I stayed here quite late tonight.

11-22-1918 There's plenty of work and little time for myself these last few days. This afternoon I wrote to M. Poinet, E. Martin and a card to Norton Company. I received three more letters from my girl today, dated July 20, July 28, and August 2nd. I had lots of good news and felt so blue and lonesome. This evening I had plenty of company to pass the evening. I am in charge of the infirmary here, over three mad Sergeants. I retired about eleven bells quite tired.

11-23-1918 The daily routine was the usual. It's a nice day today with plenty to do, such as getting the men to clean up for inspection in the infirmary. Things are looking neat here now – we passed good A #1. This afternoon there was a little paperwork to do. This evening was a lonesome one for me, although so many came into the office and saw my girlie's picture on my desk. It makes me think of many things and of our good times in the past. I retired quite late and am not feeling entirely well.

11-24-1918 Sunday. There was no reveille today. I got up an hour later, then ate breakfast and went to the infirmary. I washed and shaved and cleaned up for the day. Then duty for the day began. It's a beautiful day before us. There are plenty of Russian soldiers here in this place. They are a hard looking set of men and very dirty and lousy. Whew! This afternoon was paperwork making preparations for moving to the other pen (penitentiary). I made a sketch this afternoon on the layout of our new infirmary. I saw Sergeant Searles today. I owe him fifty francs so far. This evening I spent writing to my girlie over there #62 letter. I answered those I last received.

[To reiterate I think Walter was a draftsman besides an artist, and possibly an engineer, which would account for his being put in charge of all of this. He certainly was good at paperwork and writing. In addition he spoke German.]

11-25-1918 I neglected my diary today. We are making preparations to move our company to Prison enclosure #2. It's a rainy sloppy day. I worked hard all day.

11-26-1918 We moved our infirmary over to Prison #2 this morning after sick call. There was plenty to do. I had charge of the whole job. I was busy all day. We have got a better place now and I arranged things to suit myself. It's a very bad day today. Our Company also moved over to new barracks, while the French took over our old place at 2:00 P.M. this afternoon.

11-27-1918 We had orders to roll our packs to move out, but since transportation is blocked so much, we will have to wait until a later date. I am still in charge of the place. We changed the old Germans for new ones, since their company is going to leave soon. Things were surely upside down but were soon straightened out before sick call this morning. I retired very late this evening.

11-28-1918 Today is Thanksgiving Day. Two years ago comes to mind now. It's a rainy, sloppy day. It's lonesome and dismal for me, especially with memories of the past hitting me hard. We had a very good supper tonight with a speech from our beloved Captain, the best I've ever had. Tears came to my eyes tonight while thinking of those at home. We had a wild time tonight and the infirmary was a busy one also.

11-29-1918 We got the old bunch back again, for they were the best we've had. They know the ropes much better, so they relieved them. Things are running along smoothly again. It's a rainy sloppy day. There's nothing but a busy day, interpreting, etc. I retired quite late.

11-30-1918 It's my birthday today - I'm 25 years old. I'm getting old, but I still feel like I'm twenty. We had an inspection this morning here in the infirmary. The weather cleared up a bit today. I worked pretty hard today, the same as other days. I retired late tonight.

12-1-1918 It's Sunday and this was an easy day for me. I cleaned up things around the place. I took the afternoon off, but didn't enjoy myself very much because things don't feel the same as at home. I came back and wrote #63 letter to my girlie. It was a wild time on the other side of the barracks tonight as they were suffering from drink. They had to extract a Russian. Then I retired for the night.

12-2-1918 It's a fair day today. I'm going through the same duty as preceding days. Things are going along nicely. It's a good system we have here. I went to bed quite late as the boys and I were sitting around telling stories, etc.

12-3-1918 The weather was undecided – it was foggy this morning. I worked hard all morning on the same daily routine, etc. This evening I felt foolish and raised the dickens with the boys here in the infirmary.

12-4-1918 It's a sloppy day today. Sick call was big today, mostly from influenza. I sent two to the hospital. I was here all day busy as a bee, typewriting, paperwork, etc. We're making ready to leave soon. Captain Linderman and Captain H.M. Ross are the doctors here now. Two letters came today from my girlie #68 and #71 dated November 12, 1918. I also got two from the Reagans. Tears were in my eyes when I read these letters, because I was so happy. I went over to see Sergeant Searles tonight and had a good time.

12-5-1918 I got up about 8:30, but mustn't say this: I've been getting away with it since this job came into my hands. This morning brought me happiness, letters #56, #57, #58, and #59 from Norma arrived finally. She sent two dollars in this bunch. I also received two letters from Aldrich, one from Pop, and one from Ed Martin. I was a busy boy reading my mail this morning. The letters were such wonderful ones from my Norma the dear girl. Today I sent one prisoner with mumps to the hospital. We sure are the ones who are getting soaked for what we buy in France, since we are Americans.

12-6-1918 I got up about the usual time and dressed. Sick call was at the usual time. We move tomorrow, so I must make preparations for this occasion, packing the medicals, etc. I'm going to lose my good job here and go back into the ranks again. It's just the way things are, with no chance at all. This afternoon the Sergeant here and I went to Souilly and looked the place over. This was my first chance to get a little time for myself. It's a beautiful warm day. I took sick tonight with a slight fever. I doctored myself tonight to check as best I could.

12-7-1918 I got up about 4:30 A.M and rolled my pack and made ready to move from Souilly to St. Pedmore with some 450 prisoners. We started our trip to the rail head and arrived here about 5:50 A.M. It's a misty muddy day for traveling. I got the same accommodations as before on the freight cars. We were glad enough to leave here on most anything. The prisoners were also happy. Everything went in good order as we started on our humpty dumpty trip about 8:30 A.M. So now we're off and not interested enough for the site seeing part of the trip. When night came, I was on guard from 4:30 P.M to 8:00 P.M. Then the guard was taken off and the doors locked. There's not much sleep on this trip.

12-8-1918 I didn't know much of what happened today, for I was in a different kind of feeling. I sure did kill some of my discouragement today - all right? I had the time of my life as crazy as I was with all the risky things I did, jumping from one car to another. I almost lost the train one time when the train stopped. I had some time in the automobile on a flat car with Sergeant Bailey Dixon.

[I find it really hard to believe that my grandfather was being so reckless – I never knew him to act like this. Perhaps he needed to release all the stress he had stored up from being away from home so long and witnessing all the horrors of such a terrible war, to say nothing of being nearly killed.]

12-9-1918 We pulled into our destination early this morning. Oh, my, what a feeling!? We will leave the cars about 5:30 A.M for our destination with prisoners to the C. Penitentiary. My, my, but that pack was heavy this morning. We turned the prisoners over and we were then given breakfast here. We sure were somewhat of a dirty bunch – it sure was a scream to look at the dirty faces. We were then given tents to bunk in and we're here for an indefinite period. I was pretty much disgusted tonight. I ought to write to my Norma tonight. I wonder what she can be doing tonight? dear girl. I looked over her pictures tonight on my bunk before going to bed.

12-10-1918 It was raining this morning at reveille which was at 5:45 A.M. I was pretty stiff and sore this morning from laying on damp ground. I answered sick call but only got pills for this. Some doctors here?! I'm getting ready to go on guard here at 11:00 A.M . This is my first guard duty for some time. I have got No. 8 Post 2 relief T section at the P.W. Warehouse. It sure did rain hard this afternoon but didn't last long. It cleared up and the sky was fine. After supper, the stars were shining brightly. I will start my letter to Norma tonight, but will not send it until tomorrow.

12-11-1918 I went on guard from 1:00 to 3:00 A.M. While on guard, I went over my past thinking of all the many things I went through, etc. up to the present day, including all the foolish things that I've been doing too. I returned to the guard house and slept until the next relief which is at 7:00 until 9:00 A.M. It sure did rain all morning and we have miserable weather before us today. I was relieved by another guard at eleven bells and then came back for dinner. After dinner, I cleaned my rifle which needed it badly. Then I had a haircut for which I owe the barber – a total of five francs so far. It's still raining hard. I must finish the letter I started last night #64 to Norma which I sent along with two poems and a letter from Pop enclosed. I answered Ed Martin's letter of August 16th.

12-12-1918 Reveille was at 5:45 A.M. with arms this morning, getting in discipline around this camp. I policed around the place, then washed up and laid around. I went over and had Lieutenant Riviness censor my letters to Norma. He didn't look at them - I'd rather he didn't. He's a good old scout at that, very sociable. I hit him for a pass to Tours which I got. I also saw Sergeant Searles this morning and he gave me several Worcester papers to read. It's raining again today. After noon mess as I was getting ready for my trip to Tours, on my way I saw Charlie Simmons. I sure did have a long chat with him. Then I went and had a good time in Tours. Some place! I enjoyed myself pretty well and got back about 11:30 P.M. I saw a good show for the first time that was real vaudeville.

12-13-1918 Reveille was at 5:30 A.M. as usual. Getting up in the dark isn't any fun. I policed the place and then laid down for a while, as I didn't get much sleep last night. I am tent orderly this morning. I was on detail getting rations. When I finished this, I came back to my bunk. I was handed two letters, #62 from Norma dated September 6 and the other from Reagan dated November 14. The one from Norma gave me happiness, for it had sixteen pages to it with a dollar inside and clippings of Norma. Afternoon retreat was at 3:55 P.M. Then we fell in for mess. It's a half decent day today. With the money Norma sent me I went to Tours again and invested in a new cap. Since I had some time all by myself, I went to the A.E.F. Show. Two passes in succession is going some!!! Then I came back about 11:00 P.M. and went to bed.

12-14-1918 Reveille was at 5:30 A.M. After mess, I made my bunk and policed up the tent. I answered sick call this morning – was marked for quarters, have a chaffed___? No fun. I sewed on my emblem of the "D" this morning. I stayed in my tent all morning until dinner mess. We have pretty good grub here - no kicks. After retreat, mail call blew here again. I was made very happy with #70 letter from Norma dated November 1 with my birthday card from my girlie and a sweet message on "the card." I also got two letters from Erhard dated September 25 and November 14 which were very good letters. I got a very nice letter from cousin Estelle dated October 5 with a big letter X at the end and one from Travis with a card, five letters in all – that's going some! I am sending #65 letter to Norma today. I also sent Estelle's letter to Norma to read. I spent all evening alone in the tent with the mail in front of me, writing eighteen pages to my girl. Now for bed – it's quite late. Although we're still in tents, it was a very pleasant and warm evening for writing.

[A big letter X was meant to be a kiss.]

12-15-1918 Reveille was at the usual hour. I policed around my bunk. Then I went to sick call and was marked for quarters today. I shaved and cleaned up, then stayed around my bunk. It's a beautiful warm day today with the sun at its best again once more. I had Norma's letter censored and sent on its way. We had a fair dinner today. I dressed up this afternoon in the best I've got. I got a pass from Lieutenant Rivinus today to go to Tours. After retreat and supper, I started on my trip and went with the intention of seeing Simmons, but he wasn't in. Guess he's having <u>some</u> <u>time</u>. I was all alone in Tours, lonesome as the deuce, so I started back early. On my way back, my experience started as a French whore came up to me and asked me to —— her. Would you believe it? It took all my will power to hold my own! I thank God for that and my Norma too! I retired early.

12-16-1918 Reveille was at the usual hour. Breakfast mess was fair. I came back to the tent, cleaned up, made my bunk and policed around the tent. I am on guard roster today, so I am making preparations for inspection, etc. This comes at 11:00 A.M. Today is misty and dismal. I was picked out by an officer to act as orderly at the office. I never expected this and my Bunkie was also picked by another officer. It sure did look funny to the other boys that it came out this way. It turned out to be a very nice and busy day for me. This will bring me another pass after I am relieved from this duty. After I got through with my duty tonight, I sat down to the typewriting machine and wrote a letter #5 to Erhard, only a short letter, answering his last two.

12-17-1918 I came on duty at 8:30 A.M. and worked the same routine as yesterday. It's another nice day today. I had the pleasure of meeting Lieutenant Jones from Company C of my old regiment today. He's spending a few days with Sergeant Searles. I was relieved at 11:00 A.M. and then given a pass to Tours. I got twenty francs from Sergeant Searles, which now makes seventy francs I owe him. I went to Tours with the intention of having my pictures taken, but didn't have enough money to pay for them. I had a splendid time, better than I had in all my times in Tours, for I had some French wine. I had some head tonight and was stopped several times by French mademoiselles for something I could not do. It was a beautiful moonlight night, a night that brought my memories back to my old hometown and Norma.

12-18-1918 Reveille was at the usual hour. I didn't have breakfast this morning. It's a very disagreeable day, misty and rainy, going to be a pip – I feel it in my leg. Oh, what a rotten day, some place, this tent leaks like a sieve! I policed around the tent and my bunk for the company inspection. This afternoon I fooled around my bunk, making it as comfortable as possible. At retreat tonight we went to the location where we were getting out of here to be sent to St. Aignan. Then we were put into companies of 150 men to be shipped to the Base Port for Home, Sweet Home. This put a happy feeling on all of us boys. I will start a letter #66 to Norma. I received a letter from M. Poinett and Mrs. Reagan, as well as two cards from Mr. & Mrs. Reagan. I wrote to M. Poinett also.

12-19-1918 Reveille was at 5:45 A.M. It's still raining but it's going to be a good day. A little chilly this morning but the sun is now shining. I cleaned up and shaved this morning, then policed around my bunk. I brought the two letters over to the office to be censored by Lieutenant Rivinus. I got a pass to Tours from him. We had a fair time in this place of Tours. We came back long after the A.E.F. show was over. Then we went to bed.

12-20-1918 Orders came in about dinner time to get ready for St. Aignan, a step nearer home. We left here at 1:45 P.M. on freight cars, a two-hour run to the place where we get off. Here is O.K. We laid around until our billets were found and then we had mess. Whew! What a mess line! I came back and went to sleep. Some mob here!

12-21-1918 We got up about 8:00 A.M. Then we fell in to go through the Mill here at the Classification Camp. First we went through the U.C. Office, then through the delouser, and then had a bath. It takes about three hours to go through this mad house. After tussling through this, we were then given a billet for the night. There were no bunks so we slept on the ground. It's a rainy night to be sure, as luck would have it. I was where it was dry anyway. We had a few glasses of beer at the café. I helped an unlucky fellow that fell down and ran his hand into a nail on a board. I took him over to the infirmary where he was treated. Then I came back and went to bed. Feeling good?

12-22-1918 I got up for breakfast and then rolled my pack and made ready for the flat foot farm I was at before. I dread going there. We came here in trucks from St. Aignan in the morning at about 9:00. It's some muddy hole, a place where it's bound to rain most all the time. We laid around here some time before we got orders to even make our tents. I am in the 8th Receiving Company here. We pitched our pup tents out in the large drill field. It sure was hell to sleep on the ground, but we managed to keep warm with three of us in the tent: Blackburne, Bermby and myself. I was in the middle. I found out they are taking no more outgoing mail.

12-23-1918 We got up and out to mess. It's raining again today. Then we came back and all went to work on the big tents. We worked all morning until noon mess. When we returned, we resumed the same job we had in the morning. Of course, the 8th Company gets plenty of details. After the tent for our company was pitched up, we struck our pup tents and moved to these last ones built. I made my bunk but there's no straw so I will do the best I can without it. It will be a cold night, very damp and wet. I passed a miserable night, pretty nearly frozen to death. This isn't right the way conditions are here!

12-24-1918 I got up at the usual hour. Then I was detailed to carry lumber for a new mess hall. Then we had more tents to put up for others to move into. This company is sure getting a rub on details. This sure is some mad house all right! The night before Christmas? Oh, yes!

12-25-1918 I got up this morning for mess which will be served at 7:00 A.M. Some day! No Christmas for me or any of the boys here! I have a sad feeling with my little girl back there and I cannot even write to her at this place! I wonder how she is enjoying this day back there. What a disgusting feeling! I went for a walk all alone this evening to be alone with my "girlie". What a feeling – nobody knows but I do.

[This is his second Christmas away from home. I'm pretty sure the German celebrations were similar to the Scandinavian. At least it would have been for the Kriegers, because their step-mother was Scandinavian. Our Christmas celebrations always began on Christmas Eve with a Swedish smorgasbord dinner with the extended family. This was traditional among Scandinavian families: boiled lutfisk with melted butter or mustard sauce, and boiled potatoes. The menu also included pickled herring, pickled beets, liver pate, boiled potato and pork sausage, Swedish meatballs, red cabbage, hard tack, Swedish coffee bread (Norma made the best), and Christmas rice porridge with cinnamon and milk (Norma made the best). Julglogg made from red wine with cardamoms, cloves, almonds, raisins, bitter orange peels, figs, and cinnamon stick was served for the adults. We had a Christmas tree decorated with straw decorations imported from Sweden, and tomtes, which were little elves decorated with fur and hats made of knitted yarn also imported from Sweden. There were also Swedish dala horses (painted wooden horses) and large goats made of straw with red ribbons. On Christmas Day we opened our brightly wrapped gifts and then had a Christmas ham with mustard, apple sauce and stewed prunes, mashed potatoes, red cabbage, carrots, and peas. Of course, we had Swedish pepparkakor (very thin ginger snaps, which Norma made best) and Swedish spritsar cookies made with lots of butter and almonds shaped through a machine into various shapes (which Norma made the best). Swedish coffee bread, Christmas rice porridge and Julglogg was served again. We always went to church either on Christmas Eve at midnight or early on Christmas morning. Can you imagine missing all of this for two years in a row? Poor Walter. Poor Eugene.]

12-26-1918 I got up for breakfast. I wasn't feeling supreme this morning. We put up more tents today. A bunch left here for the states – a happy bunch of boys, the same as I myself will be when I leave this hell hole! I returned quite late. Some head?

12-27-1918 It's the same sloppy day as yesterday. I never saw the best of this place – it's always bound to rain, making the day miserable for all of us. We will all be glad to get out of this place. I retired feeling disgusted. I hope nothing has gone wrong at home.

12-28-1918 I got up in time for chow. Then I policed up, cleaned etc. I did a few details this morning. Nobody is going out today. About 2:30 in the afternoon we had dinner. We had a lot of trouble about messing. I was feeling miserable all day. I went over to the café and drank some wine. Some head?

12-29-1918 I got up at 9:00 A.M. Then I went to mess. It's a misty dismal day. The tents we are in were moved today twice. We lined them up by the first one. We had dinner about 4:30 today – only two meals all day – going some! I spent the evening in the tent, made my bunk and laid down. We sang together – a violin played all the songs. Then we told stories. I heard some good ones! At taps things got quiet. Now I'm going to say a prayer for my girl.

12-30-1918 Today is my brother Gene's birthday. I got up at reveille and went to mess, such as it was. Some day – it rained, rained, rained - an all day thing. We evacuated some of the boys today. Some boys from Massachusetts that were sent away before were sent back here again. Dinner was served at 2:30 P.M. Some soaking wet day! This evening my bunk mate Cadd was taken away sick. Comy was then my new bunk mate.

12-31-1918 My, what a day it is – rained like hell at reveille! Mess was rice, syrup, bread and coffee. We spent all morning in the tent waiting for evacuation any day. It seems to be all politics the way things are run! Dinner was slim – nothing much! Only two sticks of wood are allowed for two stoves, when it is issued to us. There was some hissing when these orders were read! This sure has got all places beat – the boys will never forget the swell treatment at the flat foot farm now used for an evacuation depot! Supper – our last one this year – sure was a swell one at that! O-N-E P-I-E-C-E O-F B-R-E-A-D and A C-U-P O-F C-O-F-F-E-E. It's getting worse and worse! To enjoy the evening the best way possible I took in the show at the YMCA hut. I had a fair time tonight. I made a good sketch on my way, which is almost a kilometer to the tent. I spent the time "talking" to my girl. I was walking toward the west all the while "talking" to her (dear girl). Too bad she couldn't hear me! Now I must retire for the night, hoping to be home early next year. This completes my whole year's experience in France without a slip or much neglect towards my diary. Now for bed and a prayer for my girlie.

1-1-1919 Three years ago I started to go with Norma. The time sure does fly. I got up this morning about 8:30 A.M . and went to mess. All morning I laid down thinking of my past and future, hoping to be sent home soon. It is a fair day, but cloudy. For dinner we had S.O.S. as any other day's slum, our New Year's dinner on the Flat Foot Home! I cleaned up a bit and then went for a short walk up the road. Afterwards, I wrote to Norma. Mess time came, but what a "mess" it was: "goldfish" mixed with onions, bread and coffee! After eating, Sanford and myself went for a walk and ended up at the Y.M.C.A. and took in the show. We saw a Russian dance by one of the "Y" girls who was very prettily dressed. We came back and retired for the night. For a wonder, things were pretty quiet in the tent tonight. I said my prayers and went to sleep.

[S.O.S. is creamed chipped beef on toast. I believe it is short for "sh__ on a shingle" according to my husband who was in the National Guard, but I'm not sure.]

[Slum is short for Slumgullion, which is a thin beef stew with onions and tomatoes and seasoning. Sometimes Doughboy cooks added a crust over the cooking stew or crumbled hardtack to create Full Pack Slum.]

1-2-1919 Early this morning a gale wind blew and many of our tents got a knock down. Of course, the one I was in had to blow down. The bunch in the tent sure did hate to get up at this time more than anything else which was about 2:00 A.M. (There were more arguments as to who was going to get up and fix the tent.) Comy and myself didn't care much whether we were outside or not. We got up maybe about 6:30 A.M . I didn't eat cornmeal which is what is mostly served in this camp in the morning. I ate the one slice of bacon they gave us, the bread and the coffee. We all had to make a change with tents this morning again. We lined up three of them. Dinner was slum (a thin stew), one spud and coffee. During the afternoon, those who didn't duck the detail this morning were let out of working. So I shaved and cleaned up with the afternoon to myself.

1-3-1919 I got up for breakfast and was then on detail policing around the place. It rained to beat the band all morning. Gee, what a place for rain! I am having trouble about the mess every day here. It cleared up for a short while and rained again about dinner time just when a fellow has got to eat.

During the afternoon, it cleared up for a while. The afternoon was spent in the tent. I was pretty sore as the rest of the boys were discontented with the conditions here in the camp. Suppertime came and more rain with it. The evening was spent discussing several things concerning different matters regarding the conditions in this camp. It was early when I rolled over and went off to dreamland.

1-4-1919 I got up for breakfast, cleaned up and performed the same routine as any other day. It was quite pleasant this morning, but something terrible happened this afternoon. The kitchen sure did catch hell, for they didn't have things ready for the men. It wasn't until 4:00 P.M. that they served noontime dinner. It was almost a mutiny that started in this camp. The men all hollered, "When do we eat with the S.S. added? Throw away your mess kit!" We all got a speel from our Lieutenant who tried to explain to us what the trouble happened to be. I fell in for seconds – managed to squeeze in just in time! We sure were a hungry lot. I came back and passed the rest of the time on my bunk and went to bed for the evening.

1-5-1919 Sunday. I got up for breakfast mess and then cleaned up and policed the tent etc. Then the Company fell in for a stiff lecture by the officers here concerning the mess proposition and also the wood and water supplies. Gee what a balling out we got from the officers for yesterday's trouble. Dinner was served on time with another formation for roll call at 3:00 P.M. We had a formation on drawing blanket, and another on who stole the watch. This was some way to spend Sunday. As usual it rained off and on today. Supper was on time – we had "goldfish" for this meal. After supper, I went down to the woods and stole some wood for the stove. I retired early tonight. There is another gale wind blowing tonight. I hope the tents don't blow down again. Now for some sleep.

1-6-1919 Reveille formation this morning and then show call for mess. It was a fair mess this morning. It's a fair but windy day. We fell in for drill today and setting up exercises. We were put into squads – I'm in the first squad, my old place. We returned from drill in time for dinner. We had slum again which was bum too. There's nothing satisfactory here at all. We had formation after dinner and thought we were out for a hike, but when we reached the supply house things changed. We were halted here and marched over to draw bunks for the non-commissioned soldiers. This was using good judgement. I guess that the men who rightly belong to these bunks should be the wounded men. I suppered and then scouted up some wood for the evening. Then I retired.

1-7-1919 We had reveille, but I couldn't get my shoes on today. So I had no breakfast this morning. It's very windy out today. I stayed on my bunk all morning. It was evacuation day today for a number of men, but not me. My friend Gaughn went out today. I walked to mess in stocking feet. We had slum again for dinner. I spent the afternoon as I spent the morning. I played rummy for a little while. My bunkie Comy left me for somewhere else, but I don't know where yet. Supper came and then I went for a canteen of water. I came back and laid down on my bunk ready for bed. I retired early. Colonel Roosevelt died today at 4:15.

1-8-1919 There was reveille again but not for me because I couldn't get my shoes on. I went to mess in stocking feet again. We had oatmeal, syrup, bread and coffee. I came back and made my bunk up new again. I can't account for much today. It's a beautiful day – something new for this place! This Company is on detail for today. Dinner was slum, bread and coffee. I spent the afternoon on my bunk. I can hear a band playing in the distance. Nobody leaves here today. I spent the afternoon on my bunk. The boys bring their wood to get warm. I went to bed early.

1-9-1919 We had reveille but I didn't get up for this formation. I went to breakfast in my stockings again. It's a nice day today. I laid around on my bunk all day with nothing to do but think about going home. I can not write any letters. Dinner was served and again I spent the afternoon on my bunk. I got a new pair of shoes today, size 10E. There was a bum show at the Y.M.C.A. I went for a short walk before going to bed. It was a lovely night with a nice moon. I went to bed early again.

1-10-1919 Reveille was at the usual time. Mess time came around. I policed and cleaned up. We have to roll down the sides of the tents at this time of year as it's pretty cold here now. It is a cold, windy day. There was nothing much for today, but miscellaneous details. Comy, my Bunkie, leaves me today. I went to bed early.

1-11-1919 Reveille was at the usual hour and then mess. I policed the tent, chopped wood for the stove for tonight. We have a bad misty day before us. I have a new Bunkie now, but actually he's one I had before named Cadd. He's a pretty good scout. After supper, we came back, made the bed, and played a few hands of whist tonight. It was a hot game.

1-12-1919 Sunday. There was no reveille today but I got up for mess It is a peach of a day. We completed the fronts of our tents with the decoration. Ours is a beautiful piece of work. The Lieutenant came through the camp inspecting for the best looking piece of work. Our tent had the best decoration so we were given first prize. It was a small prize of a package of cigarettes. The Company street sure does look swell with all their decorations. We were complimented by the Major of this Post. Only two meals were served today. In the evening it rained pitch forks so we stayed in the tent. We went to the movies here – they were fair. We stood in the rain watching them. I came back and said my prayers. Then I went to sleep.

1-13-1919 Reveille was at the usual time and then mess was served. It's a beautiful morning. I'm going through the same daily routine as before. I'm waiting to get out of this hole. A few names were called for people leaving today, but I was not amongst them. I suppered and then wrote a letter to my girlie over there, taking a chance that the letter would go through the mail. I sent a few cards also to Erhard Kjellberg, Charles Krieger and Pop Krieger.

1-14-1919 I got up bright and early. After breakfast mess I came back and policed the tent. The men argued on who was to get the wood today. At about 9:00 A.M . there came an evacuation order and I was amongst them. "Hooray!" I yelled, " At last!" We were taken down to St. Aignan on trucks. I am in a Company here known as the 409th Company ready to leave in a week's time. We were put in squad tents here amongst other boys. I was in H Company Street here. About noon I met Booton and was surprised to be handed about 19 letters for me. Gee, I was in luck all through the today.

[Throughout Walter's diary, he never mentioned that Eugene had been wounded. Apparently the newspaper article printed the information incorrectly; it was Walter who was seriously injured and Eugene slightly injured. Maybe that's why he gave his father a piece of his mind!]

The photo below was taken of ruins after the war by C.W. Robertson and provided to me by Ellen (Asplund) Racine of the Northborough Historical Society.

In the photo below Walter is on the left with three of his soldier friends.

Chapter 5:

Walter Returns Home
to Worcester, Massachusetts

Below is a photo of Norma and Walter in her father's garden after his return from France.

After Walter's return to the United States on February 14, 1919, he was honorably discharged at Fort Devens, Massachusetts. He was awarded a purple heart for bravery and due to the wounds sustained in France. Walter and Norma were married on June 1, 1920, in Central Congregational Church in Worcester, Massachusetts. Norma's father John J. Kjellberg, who was a patent maker, cabinet maker, and house builder, along with Walter, built their home on St. Nicholas Avenue in Worcester. Walter and Norma lived there until the tornado of 1953 wreaked destruction.

The photo below is Norma and Walter's wedding portrait.

Their only child, Evelyn Matilda Krieger, was born on November 18, 1923, in Worcester, Massachusetts. Walter was an adoring father who desired to have another child, but Norma had difficulty after Evelyn's birth with phlebitis in her legs and was bedridden for a considerable length of time. The type she had was dangerous and could be life threatening. Norma had a neighbor help take care of the baby. In later life Norma developed problems in her legs and had to have a leg amputated.

Photos of Walter and Norma with Evelyn

Erhard Kjellberg, Norma's mother Mathilda Kjellberg, Aunt from New Jersey holding Evelyn, Eugene Krieger, Aunt Hedwig's husband, and Walter seated in 1925

From left: Uncle, Eugene Krieger, John Kjellberg, Norma holding Evelyn, Mathilda Kjellberg. Eugene Krieger (second from left) and Norma's father John Kjellberg, Norma holding Evelyn and Norma's mother Mathilda Kjellberg 1925

Walter, Norma and Evelyn at Revere Beach

Charles Krieger, Norma, Lena Krieger, Eugene Krieger holding Evelyn, Aunt Hedwig

Evelyn M. Krieger (four years old on left, six years old on right)

Walter worked as a machinist at Logan, Swift and Brigham Company, which began business in 1898 at 75 Grove Street in Worcester. It later became U.S. Envelope Company. While employed there, WWII broke out and Walter, a soldier and patriot at heart, enlisted in the army again on April 26, 1942, at the age of forty-seven years. He was never called to active duty. Incidentally, in the German language, *Walter* means *brave* and *Krieger* means *soldier*.

Kenneth Andersen, Evelyn (Krieger) Andersen, Norma Krieger and Walter Krieger, 1944

Evelyn married Kenneth Olaf Andersen (who was born on October 14, 1924, in Shrewsbury, Massachusetts) on September 6, 1944. At the time of their wedding Kenneth was a member of the U.S. Army stationed at Fort Devens in Ayer, Massachusetts (again the 26th Yankee Division, of which Walter had been a member). Because he was blind in one eye from a childhood accident, he was never sent overseas, but served in the army in the United States in Northampton, Massachusetts, and then in Kansas. Because Carol Ann, their first child, was born in 1945 before the war ended, she and Evelyn lived for a short time with Kenneth while he was stationed in Northampton and later in Kansas. Following the end of World War II, Evelyn and Kenneth, along with their first child, moved into the upstairs of Walter and Norma's home on St. Nicholas Avenue. Their second child, Linda Jean, was born three years later in 1948.

Photo below is Walter holding his first granddaughter Carol Ann Andersen in 1945.

As a child, I used to spend a lot of time with my grandparents. I adored both of them, because they were the most patient and loving of grandparents, more like parents. Since Evelyn was an only child, she was always wishing for a brother or sister. That never happened. I felt that she treated me more like her sister than her daughter. Evelyn always encouraged me to help take care of my baby sister, Linda, which lasted into adulthood. We were an extremely close family, because of the love and care of Walter and Norma, which was transmitted to their daughter Evelyn. Below is a photo of me (Carol) with my grandpa and our two dogs after he shoveled the driveway about 1947-1948.

Lady, Carol, Duchess, and Walter playing in the snow

Below is a photo of Carol holding her sister Linda Jean Andersen in 1948

The above photo shows Norma Krieger with her two granddaughters, Carol Ann and Linda Jean, in 1950

The above photo shows Evelyn Andersen with her daughters Carol Ann and Linda Jean in 1950

The above photo shows Eugene Krieger and Walter Krieger on the steps of Walter's home on St. Nicholas Avenue

After Walter's heart attack about 1950, he took up artwork with pastels. I loved sitting with Grandpa, watching him as he created beautiful works of art, mostly scenery or animals. He would teach me why he was using different colors and how to shade things and make the painting look three dimensional. He would let me practice what I was learning from him. This lead me to a love of art and I practiced various forms of art throughout my life, eventually becoming an accomplished portrait painter using acrylic paints, thanks to Walter's early influence. When Walter was able to return to work, he became a machine operator at Worcester Envelope Company, where he worked until retirement.

The photo above is of Frodigh relatives (Norma's cousins) showing Erhard Kjellberg (Norma's brother) second from the left and Walter second from the right. Walter had a lot of friends. The photo below shows Walter with many of his friends; he's the second from the right. It looks like this was taken outside of his place of employment.

Chapter 6:

The 1953 Tornado in Worcester Changes Life for Walter's Family

On June 9, 1953, an extremely powerful F4 tornado struck Worcester and the surrounding area, staying on the ground for about ninety minutes, covering about forty-eight miles of territory from Petersham through Barre to Worcester to Shrewsbury to Westborough, until it dissipated in Framingham. It was part of the Flint-Worcester low-pressure tornado outbreak sequence that occurred from June 6-9, 1953, wreaking havoc from Colorado, Kansas, Nebraska, Iowa, Michigan, and Ohio, traveling across the Great Lakes area into Pennsylvania, New York, New Jersey into New England, and touching down again in the Quabbin Reservoir in Petersham. New England had never had a tornado before that occurrence, and although the National Weather Service informed Boston of a possibility for tornado activity, they never included it in their weather forecast. By the time the tornado reached the Worcester area particularly the Burncoat Hill and Uncatena Avenue-Great Brook Valley area, it had reached an F5 intensity. St. Nicholas Avenue where the Kriegers and Andersens resided was between Uncatena Avenue and Great Brook Valley, where the greatest devastation occurred.

About 5:00 P.M. after I arrived home from school, I was standing in the window watching the thunderstorm swirling around us outside and saw the tops of the trees literally touching the ground. I also heard a frightening sound as loud as a freight train, like we were standing right next to it. I related this to my mother Evelyn, who was watching television with my sister Linda. She immediately became alarmed and yelled to me to get away from the window and grabbed Linda and me and dragged us through the doorway just as the living room ceiling collapsed. At that precise moment Walter arrived home from work, yelling to all of us to get down cellar, that it was a tornado. Since he had been stationed in the southwest, he knew very well what a tornado happened to be. As we flew down the stairs, glass was flying all around us, cutting into our flesh. We all huddled down cellar, but the horrible sounds had subsided. When we dared to emerge from the cellar and look over our property, we saw that the next door neighbor's house was gone and her roof lay on top of Walter's car. It must have happened just after he got out and ran into the house. It was the roof that had hit the side of our house, causing the upstairs living room ceiling to collapse. We would all have been killed if Walter hadn't sounded the alarm! Once again, he was a hero!

How our house remained on its foundation when those around were gone, I'll never know. Perhaps our Heavenly Father was watching out for us! He was also watching out for our next door neighbor, who had closed herself in her closet, saving her life. Kenneth arrived home from work shortly after this. He related horrible sights, which confronted him on his walk home about one mile from Burncoat Street. He had to leave his car there due to debris and trees and bodies all over Clark Street. Imagine his relief when he saw that we had all survived with only minor injuries. The National Guard arrived that evening, helping bandage the wounded and move those critical to hospitals. In addition they provided us with food for a couple of days. Walter's brother Eugene came to check that the family was all right. The soldiers kept saluting him, which I found curious. Later Walter told me he looks just like General Dwight D. Eisenhower, who was also president at that time and the soldiers thought that's who he happened to be.

The above photo shows how totally demolished Walter's car was from the tornado. He had just exited it when the neighbor's roof crushed it.

Our house on St. Nicholas Avenue in Worcester, Massachusetts, after the devastation of the F5 tornado June 9, 1953

The above photo shows Norma's brother Erhard Kjellberg outside his house after the tornado with a carpenter repairing the roof. The entire second floor was torn off.

After the 1953 tornado in Worcester, Massachusetts, Walter and Norma moved to Holden, Massachusetts, and my mother Evelyn and father Kenneth, along with my sister Linda and I, moved to Brierway Drive in southwest Worcester. On school vacations and weekends my mother, Linda and I visited our grandparents Walter and Norma in Holden and played with the neighboring Asplund children, particularly Linda, who was my age, and Ellen, who was Linda's age. That was how I met John Asplund (Linda and Ellen's older brother) whom I married on April 2, 1966. While living on Brierway Drive, my father Kenneth began drinking alcohol uncontrollably and became abusive. After six years of abuse, my mother Evelyn, my sister Linda, and I moved in with my grandparents once again, in Holden this time. Kenneth came to Walter and Norma's home to retrieve his family. Walter confronted him and said, "My girls are staying here. You are *not* going to abuse them any longer!" Linda and I were sitting on the stairs up to our bedroom listening to the exchange. Both of us agreed, "Grandpa is our hero!"

Walter with his Krieger girls Linda, Evelyn, and Carol

The family in Holden in 1958. From left: Carol, Linda, Norma, Else Tatro (Norma's best friend), Helen Kjellberg, Erhard Kjellberg and Walter Krieger. Evelyn took the photo.

The photo below shows Norma and Walter Krieger in 1958, just a few years before his stroke. In the background is a portrait that Walter did of one of their dogs.

Walter suffered a stroke on his right side in 1960. Not only was he paralyzed on his right side, but also he could no longer speak, as speech is controlled by the right side of the brain. At the Veteran's Hospital in Rutland, Massachusetts, Walter received therapy so that he could walk with a cane. However, his ability to speak never returned. He returned home to Holden with Norma and the girls. In 1962 his condition worsened and he was again admitted to the Veteran's Hospital in Rutland.

Walter after his stroke, just before his death.

Walter died in the Veteran's Hospital in Rutland, Massachusetts, on October 31, 1962, with his wife Norma and his daughter Evelyn by his side. John Asplund had brought me to the hospital the night he passed away, but my mother and grandmother told us to leave after I said my good-byes to Walter. My first hero, my childhood hero, was gone!

As a final note, John Asplund and I had dated since 1960. Walter and John were very fond of each other. I inherited Walter's artistic ability and love of painting. I specialize in portraits, but he had taught me how to visualize and paint scenery and animals as well. I believe he taught me tenacity and perseverance through incredible odds. Although we were rather poor because of my parents divorcing when I was fourteen years old, I studied hard in school so that I graduated with high honors both in high school and college. I was able to attend a prestigious college in Worcester because of a full-tuition scholarship, and went on to earn two master's degrees. Now that I read his diary and discovered his deep faith, I believe his influence is the reason I have had deep faith my entire life.

John joined the 26th Aviation Battalion of the Massachusetts Army National Guard in 1964 during the Vietnam War. He was never called to active duty, but served in the United States for six years. So, Walter served in the 26th Yankee Division as did his son-in-law Kenneth Andersen and his grandson-in-law. I became engaged to John in 1964 and we were married in 1966 while I was still a student at Clark University. John was my second hero! Walter always desired to have a son; I wish he had lived to see his three great-grandsons, all of whom inherited his artistic ability and Norma's musical ability. All three of them became engineers: Erick an electrical engineer, Kurt a structural engineer, and Dana a computer engineer. I believe I was able to teach that tenacity and perseverance to my boys, because of how Walter taught me those skills. Incidentally, he and Norma gave us three acres of land behind their home in Holden on which John and I built a ten-room colonial reproduction home with a three-story garage and a three-story barn, which housed our construction company and equipment. It also took tenacity and perseverance for John and me to start and successfully run our construction company. None of this would have been possible without Walter and Norma's example.

Below is Walter Krieger's diary code. This is how I figured out the codes he created for each letter of the alphabet in case someone found his diary with the passwords and other personal information.

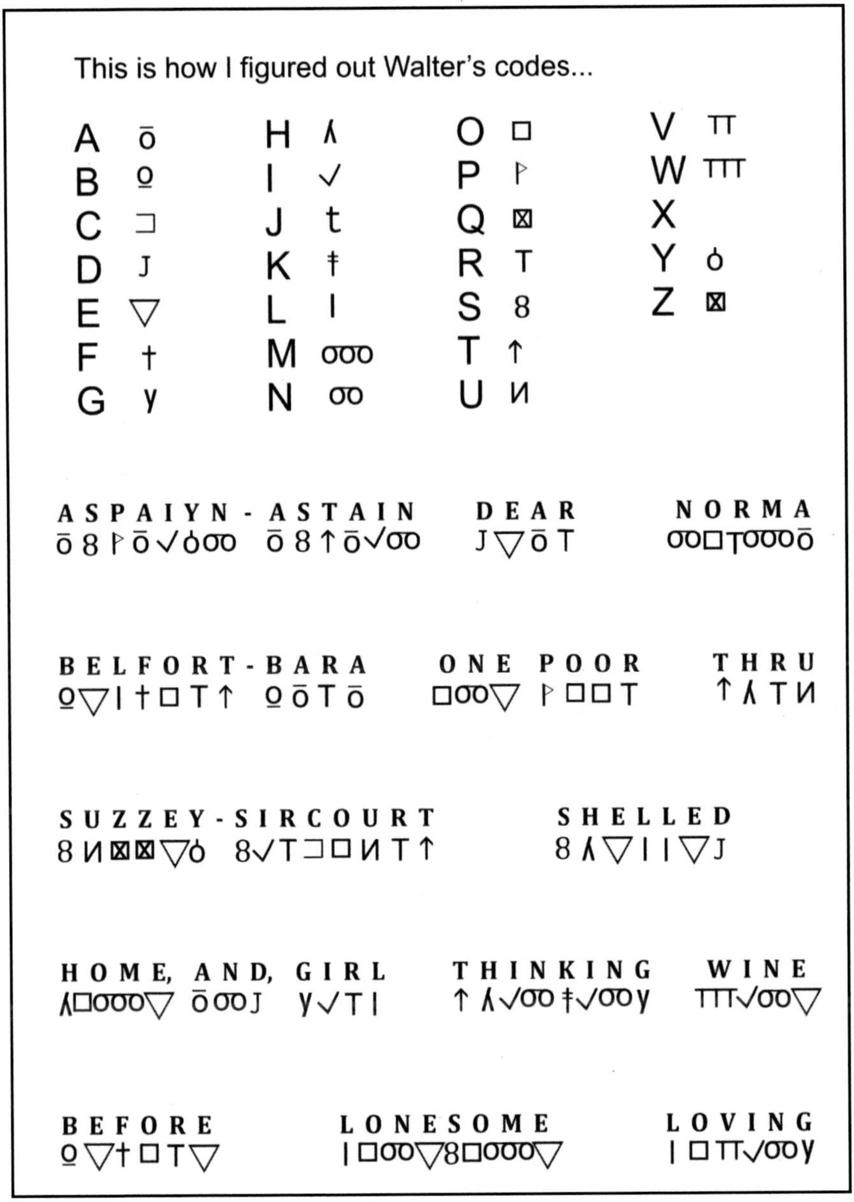

This is how I figured out Walter's codes...

A	ō	H	ʌ	O	□	V	⊤⊤
B	ǫ	I	✓	P	⸕	W	⊤⊤⊤
C	⊐	J	t	Q	⊠	X	
D	J	K	†	R	T	Y	ȯ
E	▽	L	I	S	8	Z	⊠
F	†	M	ᴏᴏᴏ	T	↑		
G	ʏ	N	ᴏᴏ	U	и		

ASPAIYN - ASTAIN
ō8⸕ō✓ȯᴏᴏ ō8↑ō✓ᴏᴏ

DEAR
J▽ōT

NORMA
ᴏᴏ□Tᴏᴏᴏō

BELFORT-BARA
ǫ▽I†□T↑ ǫōTō

ONE POOR
□ᴏᴏ▽ ⸕□□T

THRU
↑ʌTи

SUZZEY-SIRCOURT
8и⊠⊠▽ȯ 8✓T⊐□иT↑

SHELLED
8ʌ▽II▽J

HOME, AND, GIRL
ʌ□ᴏᴏᴏ▽ ōᴏᴏJ ʏ✓TI

THINKING
↑ʌ✓ᴏᴏ†✓ᴏᴏʏ

WINE
⊤⊤⊤✓ᴏᴏ▽

BEFORE
ǫ▽†□T▽

LONESOME
I□ᴏᴏ▽8□ᴏᴏᴏ▽

LOVING
I□⊤⊤✓ᴏᴏʏ

Below are photos of some of Walter's pastel paintings:

THE CONSTITUTION

BY W.

Footnotes

[1] https://en.wikipedia.org/wiki/Panco_Villa_Expedition

[2] https://en.wikipedia.org/wiki/Westfield-Barnes_Regional_Airport

[3] https://en.wikipedia.org/wiki/104th_Infantry_Regiment_(United_States)

[4] https://en.wikipedia.org/wiki/Wickes-class_destroyer

[5] https://military.org/wiki/26th_Infantry_Division_(United_States)

[6] https://en.wikipedia.org/wiki/Trench_warfare

[7] https://en.wikipedia.org/wiki/26th_Infantry_Division_(United_States)

[8] https://en.wikipedia.org/wiki/Observation_balloon

[9] https://en.wikipedia.org/wiki/Eric_Bogle.
Also https://en.wikipedia.org/wiki/Bob_Seger

[10] https://en.wikipedia.org/wiki/Observation_balloon

[11] https://en.wikipedia.org/w/indexphp?cirrusUserTesting=glent_m0&search=
movie+producers+in+1917-1918&title=Special:Search&go=Go&ns0=1

[12] https://en.wikipedia.org/wiki/Reims_Cathedral

[13] https://en.wikipedia.org/wiki/26th_Infantry_Division_(United_States)

[14] World War One: How Did 12 Million Letters A Week Reach Soldiers, BBC
News Magazine, 31 January 2014, https://www.bbc.com/news/magazine—
25934407

[15] https://en.wikipedia.org/wiki/104th_Infantry_Regiment_(United_States)

[16] https://en.wikipedia.org/wiki/104th_Infantry_Regiment_(United_States)

[17]https://en.wikipedia.org/wiki/104th_Infantry_Regiment_(United_States)

[18]https://en.wikipedia.org/wiki/104th_Infantry_Regiment_(United_States)

[19]https://en.wikipedia.org/wiki/104th_Infantry_Regiment_(United_States)

[20]https://en.wikipedia.org/wiki/104th_Infantry_Regiment_(United_States)

[21]Herbert Adams Gibbons, SONGS FROM THE TRENCHES: The Soul of the A.E.F.

NOTE: I did not quote or use any information from this source other than to check for the words to the poem "Little Pal o' Mine" attributed to David Carb of the American Red Cross in this book, which did *not* match the words my grandfather had in his diary.

Bibliography

26th Infantry Division (United States), Wikipedia,
   https://military.org/wiki/26ᵗʰ_Infantry_Division_(United_States)

104th Infantry Regiment (United States), Wikipedia,
   https://en.wikipedia.org/wiki/104th_Infantry_Regiment_(United_States)

Eric Bogle, Wikipedia, https://en.wikipedia.org/wiki/Eric_Bogle.

Herbert Adams Gibbons, SONGS FROM THE TRENCHES: The Soul of
   the A.E.F. NOTE: I did not quote or use any information from this source
   other than to check for the words to the poem "Little Pal o' Mine" attributed to David Carb of the American Red Cross in this book, which did
   not match the words my grandfather had in his diary.

Movie Producers in 1917-1918, Wikipedia, https://en.wikipedia.org/w/in-
   dexphp?cirrusUserTesting=glent_m0&search=movie+producers+in+1917
   -1918&title=Special:Search&go=Go&ns0=1

Observation Balloon, Wikipedia,
   https://en.wikipedia.org/wiki/Observation_balloon

Pancho Villa Expedition, Wikipedia,
   https://en.wikipedia.org/wiki/Pancho_Villa_Expedition

Photographs by Charles W. Robertson, 103rd Infantry, M.S. Company, American Expeditionary Forces. Provided by Ellen (Asplund) Racine, Curator
   of the Northborough Historical Society, Northborough, MA.

Photographs by Platoon Sergeant Clarence N. Nelson, Company A, 104th Infantry, 26th Yankee Division, American Expeditionary Forces. Provided by Ellen (Asplund) Racine, Curator of the Northborough Historical Society.

Platoon Sergeant Clarence Norman Nelson, World War I Diary from Jan. 1, 1918 to July 19, 1918. Provided by Ellen (Asplund) Racine, Curator of the Northborough Historical Society, Northborough, MA.

Reims Cathedral, Wikipedia, https://en.wikipedia.org/wiki/Reims_Cathedral

Bob Seger, Wikipedia, https://en.wikipedia.org/wiki/Bob_Seger

Trench Warfare, Wikipedia, https://en.wikipedia.org/wiki/Trench_warfare

Westfield-Barnes Regional Airport, Wikipedia, https://en.wikipedia.org/wiki/Westfield-Barnes_Regional_Airport

Wickes-Class Destroyer, Wikipedia, https://en.wikipedia.org/wiki/Wickes-class_destroyer

World War One: How Did 12 Million Letters A Week Reach Soldiers, BBC News Magazine, 31 January 2014, https://www.bbc.com/news/magazine—25934407

Acknowledgments

Thank you to my family, especially my husband and mother, who always supported me and encouraged me to reach my potential. In addition thank you to my friends, many of whom read my manuscript and encouraged me to publish it, and to the following people:

Sarah Snider, my writing coach from Dorrance Publishing Co., Inc., for her excellent suggestions to make my book both informative and personal.

Benjamin Altomari, Senior Publishing Service Consultant for Dorrance Publishing Co., Inc.

Melissa Weisberg, Project Coordinator for Dorrance Publishing Co., Inc.

Ellen (Asplund) Racine, who digitized my photographs to .jpg format and, as curator of the Northborough Historical Society, provided additional photographs taken by Clarence N. Nelson and Charles W. Robertson. In addition she provided additional narrative from the diary of Clarence N. Nelson, who was a member of the same infantry regiment to which Walter C. R. Krieger belonged.

Finally, thanks to Erich Uwe Jaeckel for translating parts written in German and for reading my manuscript and encouraging me to publish it.

About the Author

Carol Ann (Andersen) Asplund holds a bachelor of arts in geography with a minor in geology from Clark University of Worcester, Massachusetts; a master of arts in education from Assumption College of Worcester, Massachusetts; and a master of science degree from the civil engineering department of Worcester Polytechnic Institute in construction project management. She has worked as a regional transportation planner in central Massachusetts, a city planner in Worcester, a children and young adults with learning disabilities teacher, and a construction project manager in central Massachusetts.